Aly,

Without you none of this matters.

I remember so vividly seeing you in high school and knowing there was something drastically different about you.

The last 14 ½ years have only confirmed that.

If God doesn't reach down and heal you none of this happens. You are the lynchpin to all of this.

Just as in almost every area of your life you are the piece that makes things work. Subtract you from any one relationship or family circle and the dynamic doesn't change, it explodes.

One day in Heaven we will know the people who through you came to see a version of Jesus that made them reach out to him. I personally cannot wait to see just how long the list is. It will only be limited by how long you are on this earth.

On October 17, 2011 I heard and saw something no husband should ever see or hear.

On October 17, 2011 I heard you had cancer in your body.

On April 30th, 2012 I heard all cancer was gone.

That day is the day that made today possible. There was a great deal of fighting on your part between those two dates but you did it.

One more giant you wrestled and beat.

I cannot wait to tell our daughters about their mom.

I cannot wait for our daughters to watch their mom live it out.

Aly, you will not die.

From a husband that considers himself the most blessed man to ever walk the planet, I love you and am so thankful for you.

From G: Mom…ma – I love how you love me. You always love me. Every minute. I can't figure that out? How do you love me all the time even when I'm bad? I watched you pray in your closet so much that now I pray like that. I lay down on my face and say, Jesus please….

Vera and Lydia love you Al but when I asked them what they thought they wanted to write to you they were so overwhelmed they just stared at me. I am convinced they love you and are living the dream!

WARNING

I'm not a super polished writer. There are a pile of things I brush by and shouldn't and some that I hang out and elaborate on that I should brush over.

That's why my book is cheaper than a legit author.

What to Expect: I hope you hear my heart for hurting people. I was hurting and didn't know what to do. People matter to God so much that he sent his son to die for their sins.

While they were still sinners.

That's a big deal.

I love you and you matter!

Table of Contents

How My Wife's Cancer Healed Me

Hi, Josh Taylor here. I am a man of God, husband, dad, entrepreneur, dreamer, and self- proclaimed launcher—I love seeing people's dreams and my own realized. I love people! I love being around people and I enjoy making others laugh.

In the last 5 years, there have been many moments that brought us to our knees and the last thing we wanted to do was laugh, but God has given us joy in the most un-fun of circumstances.

Although my wife was miraculously healed of breast cancer, I felt compelled to write this book of how God healed *me* through her journey. When her cancer journey started, we were geared up to do whatever it took to have her healed. Little did I know God was working on healing me in ways I didn't even know I needed to be healed.

Whether your wife is facing cancer, you are facing cancer, going through a difficult season, or you are needing physical or emotional healing, I pray this book will bring you hope and practical resources of walking in the healing that God provides. As a pastor's son who heard truth all of my life, I realized I still had to activate that truth for it to become real in my life.

I know that God did not have my wife go through cancer only for her to be healed. Her story has brought hope and healing to thousands! The behind the scenes story has much to do with what God was doing in the background, and often times he does that. He works behind-the-scenes and I am praying that this book brings

to light all He did in me during my wife's cancer journey.

Please read along with me and allow God to begin a work

of healing in you. If you are broken, know that you are on

fertile ground to be healed. The healing is so, so sweet

after the most painful of broken situations.

Josh

Hanging On

It is crazy to be writing a book all about how I was healed through my wife's cancer. I also am going to write some about how I became I dad. You see, I didn't know if I would ever be a dad, and if I ever would be one- How would I be?

Through my wife's cancer journey, I realized I hadn't yet fully accepted Christ's love for me, so the thought of being a dad with a full God-ability to love my child with the love that he or she would need---that was overwhelming. Impossible, really.

Although I knew I had a deep desire to have children, those dreams became questioned if they would ever be realized. I watched my best friend who just so happens to be my wife fight cancer and wondered if she would live. We struggled with infertility as a by- product of her chemotherapy treatments and the struggles that come with the inability to conceive. *Then* God created beauty out of ashes. Through our cancer, through our infertility (and I say "our" because it truly was "our" journey), I became a dad.

The Lord knew in His infinite wisdom that before I became I dad, I needed to be healed of my own types of cancer. I will explain in the chapters to come. Although the healing was painful, I had to be broken in order to be healed. That process was grueling, but so worth it.

For all you men who desire to be a dad, or find yourself wondering if deep-seeded dreams will ever be realized, let me tell you that mine have been far exceeded.

Not because we have been perfect, or that our life has been without struggles. Actually it is the opposite. Because of cancer and infertility, we realized we had no control over our lives. We had to give every piece of our heart and dreams to the One who gave us those dreams to begin with. And what God did with those dreams is absolutely unbelievable. Thanks for reading my story of how God healed me. The husband/dad life is the best life.

I hate cancer. I hate infertility. I love adoption. Those first two things I hate led to one of my greatest loves. The very things you are despising right now could just be the avenues God uses to make His plan come to life. Hang on, my people. We're in this thing together.

I hope you see God's love for you. When you do it will blow your mind. Praying for you.

Chapter 1: Dating and Marrying Aly

I am not sure what made me such a heavy committer in dating so early, but that's what I was. If I liked you, then it was serious. There was no "maybe" or "kind of". As I write this, I am kind of laughing because there maybe some ex-girlfriends that might read this and chuckle thinking, "Thank goodness Captain Serious didn't see his plan through!" I look back at my past self and think, "Slow down, Josh, slow down!"

Let me backtrack a bit and tell you a little bit about mine and Aly's story. Little did I know that two devastating events in our own separate lives would bring Aly and I to a new school where we would end up meeting and beginning our relationship.

Aly grew up in Lafayette, La. She was born to Fred and Cyd Page and from everything she tells me, she had a dream of a family. A loving dad and mom. A great sister, and of course the south Louisiana fun life.

Aly's dad, Fred was a successful lawyer in Lafayette. Coming back from work one day, he was killed in car accident.

As it should, this was the beginning of forming a fortitude in Aly that I now value so very highly. Aly's family ended up moving to Monroe, La. to be closer to family.

Just about the same time, the school I was attending closed down for a few years, which meant we had to find a new school. Luck would have it (even though I don't believe in luck) that I ended up at the same school as Aly. It was devastating for Aly to leave her friends and everything she knew in Lafayette. It was devastating for me to leave the school and friends I had grown up with and start attending a different school on the other side of town.

Once again, devastating events for an 11-year-old and a 13-year-old, but those devastating events, like others led to something beautiful, our forever love.

I asked Aly out on our first date in September of 2001. Her best friend was dating one of my best friends, so it seemed to make sense. We ended up going to watch a movie on a Sunday after church and needless to say the sparks did not fly on her behalf. Let's just say they *really* didn't fly.

I became great friends with Aly's mom, Cyd. You ask why?

Because Aly wouldn't answer the phone! If you say yes to a

date, what does any male think? Well, of course that you want a second date! I am awesome. In this case, Aly did not want that. Aly was too embarrassed to tell me she didn't have feelings for me, which only led to unanswered phone calls, which led to my great relationship with Cyd, who would actually answer the phone!!! It makes complete sense that she would be embarrassed to tell me she didn't like me---it definitely would not be me that was embarrassed as I kept getting ignored!!! Women are crazy! We ended up not going on any additional dates until January 24, 2003 when we went on what we call our "second first date."

When I tell you Aly was different and is different I am making the understatement of the world. I knew Aly was drastically different than any girl I had been around. At the time I didn't have a clue what that was driven by but over the next few years it became clear. Aly had been forged in a very hot fire at a very young age.

I have heard many say that we are a product of our situation or surroundings. Well in Aly's case, that made her a workhorse. The kind that shows up every day to pull, regardless of rain or shine. One of my favorite memories of Aly was when we were on a trip during Spring Break my senior year of high school. I knew she was drastically different than other girls I had been around.

We started dating in January, so when spring break came I had already planned to go skiing in Red Lodge, Montana with some of our friends. Just so happened these friends that invited me were in Aly's class and invited her to join as well. While we were there, we were all going to bed, and as I walked by the girls' room, their door was open and a light was on. When all careless Christian teenagers would have gone to bed and not blinked (me included), Aly was sitting there reading her Bible and spending time with God. What Aly didn't know was that I had grown up my entire life with a mom that showed the same commitment. I attribute much of my success in avoiding the big failings to my mom's fervent prayer for me. I desired that in a wife. And as I said, you know me, I was always thinking relationships were serious! I say this forcing myself to laugh at myself instead of being sick with embarrassment. Oh well. If it got me her, then I'm thankful for my "Captain Seriousness".

Seeing Aly consistently spend time with God sealed the deal. She was the real thing, and that was confirmed throughout our 3 ½ years of dating.

Marriage

Aly and I were married in July of 2006. We knew early on that we did not want kids at first, but wanted to enjoy each other. We were not sure when we would kick in to having kids, but we knew we loved spending time with one another. Our marriage to start was better than we could have imagined. Many people talked to us about how the first year of marriage would be the hardest, but for us that was not the case. We had a blast, and there was very little conflict. (Maybe that was the Lord giving us that blissful year, knowing what was to come). I do not remember us talking about kids all the time. I know we have always loved kids though.

When we first were married, I lived in Alabama and then quickly received an offer to work for my favorite company in the world. Growing up, a family in our church started and still owned Skyjacker Suspensions in West Monroe, La. They are the absolute coolest company there is. I spent much of my youth watching the McCurry's (the owners) drive the coolest trucks I had seen.

We were afforded the opportunity to travel to Las Vegas and Virginia with my job. In 2007-2008 when the economy took a dive, Skyjacker was not immune to it. I was laid off in what would become a huge turning point in our life. It was true heartbreak for a man.

I realized through this lay-off that I had placed my identity in success. As I drove home that day wondering how in the world I would tell my wife what happened I truly just remember being in shock. I wasn't sure what it meant. Would we lose it all? Would Aly still love me? Would she leave me? What would my friends say?

As I sat on our couch on North 8th Street and told Aly what happened, she quickly showed her resolve. She hugged me. We cried together, and prayed like crazy for direction and provision. Our dream life had hit a bump. Within weeks, all was semi-okay again. In January of 2008, I had re-enrolled in college, and we made the decision to just be students. I took a stipend-pay coaching job at Claiborne Christian School, and Aly continued in college.

I would say we just kind of cruised along in life for the next few years, and never really talked about having children. Not sure if we were so busy that it didn't come up or if we both just knew it wasn't a good time. Little did we know that these years were preparing us for a storm that was coming. We had no idea. I know it sounds cliché, but how are you supposed to have any idea that cancer or a life-threatening illness will happen to you or someone in your family? That happens to older people or other families, surely not our own, and definitely not my wife.

Chapter 2: Finances and a Baby

Money has always been a huge deal for me. Because of financial difficulties growing up being a pastor's kid, I was determined for that to never be an issue for my family. As I described after my lay-off from Skyjacker, I was in a race to achieve and so many of my decisions revolved around money. I thought I had to achieve some marker of being "man enough" and "provider enough" that I was worthy of marriage. We almost didn't get married because finances had become such an idol for me. Aly changed all that in a phone call when she simply said, "We have enough. We have God, and we have each other." That was it. We decided we would head toward marriage and trust God with our finances.

After my lay-off, when I was coaching basketball, I realized I loved coaching. To say that we loved those kids wouldn't do the feeling justice. I had coached Junior High boys and girls for a few years, and fell in love. I fell in love with the kids and fun. I fell in love with feeling and being significant. I loved knowing that I could affect the outcome of something.

For that time in my life, coaching basketball was a great job for me, even though at times I became obsessed with it. I would stay up at all hours of the night dissecting game films, calling players, having them practice after practice---all of these things were good, but often times Aly would remind me to reign it in, as it wasn't the most important thing in the world. I just cared about those kids incredibly.

In January of 2011, we were having a great year. I was the Varsity Claiborne Christian Boys' Basketball Coach, and I had an incredible group of boys that played their hearts out. They were crazy talented. A few of our favorite kids were brothers. They were both 6'6" and had become fixtures around our house, and they were carrying the load. Then I adored a group of tenth graders that I had started coaching when they were in 7th grade. These kids mattered to us. I had seen them make accomplishments, athletically, spiritually, and just mature. In a way, I felt like a proud dad.

It was during this year that Aly and I started talking about having children. We both began feeling more ready, but finances were a hold up. I was coaching, and she was still is school. That was definitely not the financial situation I dreamed we would be in when we welcomed children. And all at the same time, I remember having an overwhelming feeling to quit my coaching job.

You may be asking yourself, "Why?" "Didn't you just have an incredible season and don't you adore what you do?" The answer is "Yes." To be honest, I remember feeling silly thinking about quitting. I just knew in my heart it was the right thing to do. Coaching had become an idol in my life, and I felt the Lord calling me away from that field of work. I was heartbroken, but none the less I knew it was what I was supposed to do. As you can imagine, quitting my job with no plan of replacing that income did not leave us in a great place of starting a family. It didn't make sense. I just had to trust God with what I know He told me to do.

All I knew is that the decision was right. As I sat with our athletic director and told him of my decision, I truly hoped there would be no fight for me to stay because I wasn't sure if he fought if I could say no more than once. He didn't fight. That hurt my pride. Even though I knew he didn't need to convince me for my own good.

I then walked into my brother's office who also happens to be the Head of School for the school I coached for and told him I was resigning. My brother had just taken over as head of school, and I had sent a piece of his puzzle off the table. I felt terrible, and worse than that, I could not give a good reason why. I just knew I was supposed to resign. I hate letting any of my family members down, and to do this to my brother killed me.

So fast forward to July of 2011 and we are vacationing with our church family. I had just quit my coaching job, Aly was about to start her PhD, and I was still trying to figure out how we would make it financially. Aly and I talked and decided it was time to start a family. No good reason why we should because by all accounts financially we were not prepared for a child by my accounts. In our entire marriage, this could have been one of the worst times for a baby financially, but we were learning that things don't always have to make sense. Following God's leading had to be above all else. And now that we have kids, we realize there is never a perfect time for a child. You do what you can do, work your hardest, and trust for God to provide.

As a man I can say there was a solid percentage of me that was saying "Let's do this", and in the back of my mind was just hoping I wasn't royally messing up. I can say this is one of the first moments I remember thinking as a husband that

I was willing to risk something for the happiness of my wife. Those are some scary moments.

Baby Trying

In August we decided we would start trying to have a baby. I wasn't sure what to expect from this change. It was like I expected something to change because now we were okay for baby Taylor to show up. Funny enough, life just kept going and we were building our house. We were building this house as a form of income, knowing we would live in it for a couple of years, then move again and prayerfully make a good profit. A couple months went by and we did not get pregnant, but I knew it would happen. I didn't doubt that.

Chapter Three: Cancer Is Never Convenient

The Call That Changed Everything.

Life was going great in October 2011. I was in my element. Since I had resigned from coaching basketball, I had a great deal more time available. Because of this, I had decided to contract this house we were building myself. Real estate is truly a love of mine. I love the game. I love the fight for a deal. I love the risk. It fits my personality.

One of the most fun things about this process in particular was that Aly and I had been able to customize this house to be exactly what we wanted. The previous year we built this same house 2 times for other people, which had enabled us to find out exactly what we wanted to do different. This house would be our own. After building some 20 or so houses, this was ours. Finally everything we had learned was going to be appreciated for the Taylors. That was fun.

We broke ground in early August, and the process was

fast. Because of one of my awesome life long mentors being an electrician, I was able to do the electrical myself. You see, with my personality all I need is for someone to say, "Yes of course you can Josh", and off I go. I walked into Mr. Martin's office (a mentor and electrician) with my house plans, and we talked and then he said, "Josh, are you wanting to wire your house?" I said "Yep." And then I asked "Do you think I could do it?" And the trouble for him started with his answer, "Yes, of course you can!"

So off I went with one simple command from Martin that I needed to come see him when we started, and he would tell me where to lay the stuff out. So I was neck-deep installing the electrical wiring for our house and to my dismay was able to finish it. Praise God! That is a miracle in and of itself. I pulled all the home runs, the relays-- everything. Come to find out later that I had messed up quite a few things. Confidence doesn't always produce efficacy. I learn much of that by experience!

The sheetrock was being taped and floated. All of the wood trim was installed, and it was time to prep for painting. All the while when our home was being built, we are still attempting pregnancy. I learned via my wife (the researcher of all things pregnancy) that one of the symptoms of pregnancy is that her breasts would be sore. Because we had started trying to get pregnant, Aly was a bit sensitive to everything and thankfully so. One day in the shower while checking to see if her breasts were sore, she found a lump in her breast. We decided to have an ultrasound done, and they assured us it was nothing.

The two options they gave us was to remove the lump and then test it for cancer or to take a needle biopsy of the lump and test that. We decided that for us we would prefer the lump be removed, just for peace of mind. This procedure was done on Friday, October 14, 2011. As Aly came out of surgery, the doctor assured us it was nothing. He was able to tell from the look of the lump during surgery that it was benign. We headed home happy and thankful as ever.

Even with the doctor assuring us it was going to be nothing, we were ready to hear the test results that the lump was benign. We knew that we would get the official biopsy results some time on Monday. That Sunday morning at church for some reason I felt that we needed to go down for prayer. Our church provides elders each Sunday for anyone to have pray for them according to their need. I cannot say that I knew something was up, but I just didn't feel right. I remember asking Aly if we could go down for prayer. She looked at me like, "Josh, it's fine. We know it is nothing." But I still pushed for us to go down for prayer, and we did.

On Monday, we knew we were going to get a call to tell us about the results of the lump. The first part of the morning was normal, and then Aly and I met for lunch. We really couldn't do anything because we were a bit anxious about the test results so we went over to the new house to begin prepping for the painters. As we started working on sanding baseboards in one of the guest rooms, Aly's phone rang.

Little did I know that in mere seconds, life was about to take a hard turn toward interesting. Aly said "Hello", and I heard a man's voice. All day we had been expecting a call from the nurse, who was female. So that caught me off guard, and after talking to Aly, it hit her the same way. I did not hear what the doctor told Aly, but she instantly went white and slid down in the corner of the room while on the phone. I sat down by her trying to console her for whatever she was hearing.

She proceeded to get off the phone and all I heard was, "He said it's cancer." I couldn't understand anything she said as she was inconsolable. After hugging her for a few minutes, I went to the back of the house and called the doctor's office for clarification. He confirmed to me that my wife did in fact have cancer. We needed to come in and meet with him, but he felt that in the end we needed to go to MD Anderson in Houston simply by what he saw the cancer to be from the biopsy.

What do you say as a 26-year-old to your 24-year-old wife who was just told she has breast cancer? I hope you have better words than me, because I didn't say anything. I just hugged her. What could I say?

My Emotions

I think back about my emotions from that point forward. Well let me backtrack to where she found the lump and had an ultrasound performed. I remember talking with my parents before the lump was removed and us all saying how crazy would it have been if it was cancer. It is interesting to talk about what could have happened if something came back bad, but it is entirely different for it to actually happen. It was simply unbelievable.

As I watched Aly's face go white at hearing the news of her diagnosis, I would say I went cold. A mix of fear, questioning, and not knowing what to do. I did not have an extensive understanding of cancer to be honest. In this case it probably protected me emotionally. I knew cancer took the lives of many people, but I did not have a great deal of knowledge about the process. I think this guarded me emotionally in the beginning.

As we sat in our guest bedroom of the house we were building, we talked for just a minute and then called our parents. I called my dad and told him, and then Aly called her mom. In a terrible twist, I thought my mom and dad were together only to find out minutes later that they were in fact not together, and my mom found out about Aly through a text from a friend. We felt terrible that my mom had not heard from us.

Aly and I had dreams of the next serious phone call to our parents might be telling them we were pregnant. I had never contemplated uttering the words, "Aly has cancer." In classic fashion, my dad was quiet and just said "I'm praying, I'll talk to you later." My mom was a bit more shocked. She wanted a grand baby not a daughter-in-law fighting for her life. I cannot imagine that.

My brother and Rachel (his wife) ended up coming over to the new house, and we just hugged and talked. I still remember just being a bit cold. I was saying my wife had cancer, but I had no idea what that meant. That night we spent time with Aly's mom, a few friends and then my lifelong friend Kyle and his wife Ashley. I can tell you out of all the things I envisioned Kyle and I doing as young boys, this was not one of them. Sitting with him after my wife was just told she had cancer. There is no way you can envision that or prepare for this type of news.

I was so lost with what to do or say that when Kyle was over, I went and showed him a new handgun my brother-in-law had given me. What timing! I truly didn't know what to do. I guess I was just trying to feel just a little bit normal.

That night as we went to bed I think I expected Aly to wake up different the next day, maybe "more cancerous"? We have talked about that since that terrible night, and we both say we had no idea what to expect. The next few mornings, we walked in the neighborhood together just talking. I don't remember what we talked about, but I just knew that the time now mattered. It always mattered. But it just seemed to matter more.

What's next?

We found out Aly had cancer on October 17th and then on the 18th, we went to the doctor's office to get more information on what exactly we were dealing with. When you hear a doctor say you should go to the best cancer hospital in the world, it can be a bit disconcerting. I still remember just going through the motions. Trying to love Aly, but I still did not understand.

The next week was spent calling and trying to get into different hospitals. As I watched my wife fight to get in to people that could help her, I simply remember being at a loss for what to do. Freaking out did nothing, and acting like it wasn't real seemed to be a more under the radar approach. So I tried that when I could. That was not the healthy way to deal with it, but some kind of denial is almost necessary to deal with the pain and shock at times. We were supposed to be in Houston on a Tuesday morning so the Sunday before that, some of our friends had a group of people over to their house to pray over us and bless us. When 60 people show up on a Sunday night to pray for you, it shows you how serious things are.

That night was great and meaningful. I still remember just being in shock that it was happening. We were at a prayer meeting for my wife because she was diagnosed with cancer. Where in the world did this come from? Is this really real? It still is unreal to think about. I don't think our minds were made to comprehend news like this.

My 27th Birthday

We headed for MD Anderson Cancer Center on a Tuesday, which just so happened to be my 27th birthday. We were with Aly's mom, Cyd for this trip. The day before we had spent in Baton Rouge getting some tests run and seeing another doctor for a second opinion. This was the first of many days where I remember it starting to feel a bit out of control. My wife was apologizing for not having a great present for me since we had a lot going on. I literally thought I was going to throw something at her when she said that! You have cancer--- disregard the birthday, woman!

This was one of the first times it crossed my mind of experiencing a *last something* with Aly. Would this be the last birthday that I had with Aly? I didn't know what to do with that. These kind of thoughts were the beginning of what I would consider to be my emotional undoing. I felt guilt. I felt fear. I felt hate. I felt like I didn't believe.

The week before we left to head to MD Anderson Cancer Center, I went to Chick-Fil-A with my brother. It was the first time I remember breaking down emotionally. We were eating, and he asked how I was doing and if I was scared. I had

23

a #1 with no pickles by the way. As he asked and I tried to answer, all I could get out was, "I don't know what is going to happen. Will she die? Will the chemo ki…", and as I said "kill" I literally choked. I couldn't speak. I couldn't breathe. A weeks worth of attempting strength fell at the table. I am sure I freaked Lee out, but oh well. Those emotions weren't meant to be held in for a week disguised with strength.

As we sat at Ruth's Chris Steakhouse for my birthday dinner in Houston with Aly's mom, I remember just being in awe. We were actually in Houston about to go to MD Anderson for my wife's cancer treatment. That night we shared a hotel room with Aly's mom and sometime in the middle of the night God woke me and said "Pray." So, after fighting for a half second, I got up and kneeled beside the bed pleading for Aly's life. I had no clue if this would do anything but I was desperate enough to try.

The Reality of Aly's Diagnosis

That first day at MD Anderson was a whirlwind. We thought going in that Aly would have a mastectomy, and hopefully avoid chemotherapy. Within the first hour, all of our hopes that this could be treated easily was out the door. They suggested we do chemotherapy first, which would be followed by mastectomy. This was real and happening fast.

Then, it felt like we kept getting bad news and more bad news. We then found out that cancer had been found in Aly's lymph nodes, which was devastating to hear. The cancer had spread. I am not sure what I was thinking during this time. I remember being at a loss for words. The speed at which the next few days went and the process that progressed is not for the faint of heart.

We entered MD Anderson Cancer Center Wednesday morning October 26, 2011 thinking Aly would have a mastectomy first and then prayerfully avoid further treatment. By 1:00pm that afternoon the plan had changed to chemotherapy first, and we learned the cancer had spread. Aly would then have a mastectomy after 6 months of chemotherapy, then 30 radiation treatments and a handful of other surgeries and procedures. On Thursday October 27th, we had to make the decision that still blows my mind.

As we sat with Dr. Morrow (Aly's oncologist), she shared that if Aly was her daughter, she would have started chemotherapy yesterday. Because she recommended that we start chemotherapy so soon, there was no time for us to do anything to protect Aly's fertility. The type of treatment that

Aly was prescribed had a high likelihood to affect her ability to have children. When she delivered this news that we did not have time to preserve Aly's fertility and the likelihood of the chemo affecting it, we were hit with another blow.

Dr. Morrow gave us a few hours to think and pray while she confirmed her thoughts of us needing to start chemotherapy immediately. As our family and close friends sat in the lobby of MD Anderson's Mays' Clinic, I stood in the corner and talked with my dad. I had literally just said out loud that I could not believe in the matter of an hour we had to make a decision of whether we would preserve fertility and put off chemo or if we would go ahead with chemo and hope and pray for the best later. As I said that, the nurse called our name to come back and further discuss preserving fertility or not.

In this meeting, Dr. Morrow confirmed her thoughts that we should go ahead with chemo on Friday (tomorrow). In a mere 24 hours, she advised we start chemotherapy! Aly and I asked Dr. Morrow and Cyd (Aly's mom) to leave and give us a second. As we stood and hugged each other alone in that hospital room the only thing I remember saying to Aly was that we would just have to believe for babies later. I told Aly that we could not have children without her here, and right now we had to put her health first. The possibility of children wasn't worth the risk of losing her. We felt absolute heartbreak. This conversation with my wife is still absolutely awful to relive and think about.

So it was scheduled. Aly's first dose of chemotherapy would be administered the next day at 1:45pm.

Chapter Four: Aly's Treatment

There we were on floor 8 of the Mays Clinic at MD Anderson waiting our turn for Aly's first dose of poison. The poison that we were praying would kill her cancer cells, but we knew had a potential of hurting all of the good in her too. They called Aly's name and off we went. That was the first time I had seen the bell.

There was a bell on the wall of the chemotherapy floor that apparently patients ring when they finish their chemotherapy treatment. We quickly realized that this was a bell that not everybody was able to ring. You have to finish the treatments to ring the bell, and sadly many do not make it to ring that bell.

As Aly layed on the bed and the nurse came in to administer the chemo, it was not as earth shattering as we thought. Needle. Bags of Meds. Nurse.

In a bit of comic relief or ultimate fear I look over and see an 8 inch "shot" sitting in the nurse's basket. As the chemo started its way into Aly, I asked the lady what that shot was for. She said that sometime when people start this version of chemo they have a reaction. They can't breathe and so this shot is for that.

Awesome. That made us feel really comfortable.

A few hours passed and it was done. Aly looked fine. Aly seemed fine. We walked out and saw the family and Aly's friends. Then we went off to eat. Just so happens some friends were in Houston, so we joined them for supper at Kona Grill. Everything seemed "normal", yet my wife had poison running through her body trying to kill cells that were trying to kill her.

In my little mind I thought the moment the medicine was in, we jumped ahead to baldness, sickness and all the other things you deal with in the process. The next morning, we just woke up. My wife looked the same. It was hard to believe anything was actually happening. But, oh my, it was.

Hair Loss

Hair loss is by far the most popular of the outwardly chemo side effects. I waited for this day. It would just be one day right?

If you have ever seen Jim Carey in Bruce Almighty and he goes from wearing a robe to instantly naked then that is the idea I had of this day. Yes, that is a heck of a comparison. I just figured that one day Aly would just wake up and all the hair would be gone (forget the naked part). This was not how it went down. Little by little it started falling out.

I do however remember the first day. We were in Houston at a hotel. I was on the couch watching a football game, and Aly got out of the bed and walked over to the bathroom mirror. She said, "Josh, come here." That was it. I knew it. As I walked over she showed me a handful of hair. That was "the day" for us.

For the next few weeks the process of Aly losing her hair was quick. In another moment I remember being in the bathroom with Aly and helping her dry her hair. It was falling out rather quickly at this point. In the middle of drying it, I hugged her and just said "I am so sorry." She then said the words that reminded me how much stronger she was than me. She said, "That's just the cancer falling out." I am glad she believed it, because I was still unhappy about the whole situation. Not that she was happy about it, but her perspective amazed me. Here she was encouraging me.

I wasn't worried about her looking pretty without hair. I was worried about what it would do to her to lose her hair. That week, Aly ended up getting her hair cut thinking it would help hide some of the hair loss. The days before the haircut she had worn her hair up with a pony tail. As her hair stylist, Stephanie, took her hair down and began to brush it, I was in complete shock. There were large amounts of hair that had decided it was time to go.

Aly came away looking beautiful as ever but as her husband I was at a loss. Was she really okay?

For Aly and her friends, they were able to joke about her wigs and have a bit of fun. I can tell you to this day it is not funny to me. I mean with 100% truth that I thought she was beautiful bald. I hated her being looked at. I hated her having to explain. I hated her not feeling normal. I was still angry at the idea of this process. Even now, 5 1/2 years later, I still find it hard to be light-hearted about her wigs as it was a physical sign of what she was going through. Before losing her hair, there was no outward sign that she was sick, and now there was. I became extremely protective of her.

The Mastectomy

After Aly underwent 16 painful rounds of chemo, it was time for the mastectomy. They were going to remove both of Aly's breasts. This was a bit incomprehensible to me. On the other hand, we both agreed that we had a bit of anger toward them because of what they were putting us through. So as incredible as they were, they needed to go.

The morning came for the surgery, and all I wanted to do was write notes to her doctor, on her breasts. You know, laying claim to them. Something like "Josh's property" or "Do not touch". I guess I could laugh more about this, as we were ready to get rid of the origin of her cancer. Losing her hair had nothing to do with the cancer. Her breasts did.

When Dr. Babiera (her surgical oncologist) and Dr. Villa (her reconstructive surgeon) arrived to start the surgery, we said goodbye, and I knew that this would be important. The piece of this surgery that was so critical to us was the results of the breast tissue. After this surgery we would know how Aly's body responded to the chemotherapy.

One of the positives to doing chemotherapy first was that we would then have the tissue from the mastectomy to test as to whether or not the disease was gone. We had to wait a week to get those results. That was one long week!

Caretaking

We were told that after Aly's surgery, she would have 5 drains. Think of orange size "bags" with tubes coming out of them. These went into 5 different spots on Aly's chest to relieve the fluid that was created during the surgery. We had to change and measure these multiple times each day. During this recovery, Aly was out of it. From the time at the hospital to the time at home. What I knew about Aly was that she wanted to be home. She wanted to recover at home and not be in the hospital.

When Aly came out of surgery and Dr. Villa came in, I had been given one order and that was to find out what she had to do to go home. The answer was: keep water down, pee, and walk. Aly accomplished those things quickly. So we headed home for what was an interesting time.

One of the powerful moments for me came the day after her mastectomy. The nurse came in to give her a shower. Aly could not do any of this herself. The nurse and I walked her into the shower, sat her down and I proceeded to give her a shower.

I didn't know I was signing up for this exactly on July 22, 2006 (our wedding date) but it became clear, that it was worth it. This woman that was helpless was my dream. There was nothing and no one better. Breasts or no breasts. Helpless or helpful. Hair or no hair. Cancer or no cancer. She was and is my dream.

When we arrived at our house, Aly walked out of the car and laid in bed. That's all she did. That was it. With the exception of going to the bathroom for the next week, Aly lived in the bed. I wasn't sure when the bandages from her mastectomy would come off, but I knew that moment was important.

During this time, God was doing a work in me that I had yet to understand. He wasn't done that day in April 2012, but as I began to uncover the work of the surgeon, I felt nothing but love for Aly. I am not sure what it was but I think my most simple description is that my heart was turned heavily toward her. Her pain. Her fear. Her insecurities.

As I looked for the first time at the place where her breasts once were, I was in complete amazement at how beautiful Aly looked. I knew in that moment that this was what healing would look like. These scars would serve as reminders of the battle that took place for Aly's body. Every time I looked at her bare chest would be a reminder of what Satan tried to do and how our God healed my wife. Pure, exceptional beauty.

This was heartache in the middle of the most incredible healing I would see. My beautiful Aly had her breasts removed, but she looked as incredible as ever.

I leaned down to kiss her chest, and I wanted nothing more than to convey to her that I thought she looked as beautiful as ever and there was no change in my view of her in our most intimate moment ever as a married couple.

A note to all men that think you can't act on your desire to do right even when you have done wrong, that is incorrect. Do right. I, at times can be hard on myself and believe the lie that I am not good enough to do right for the things I have done wrong. That is a lie, and that moment where I allowed God to intervene through me is a moment that is incredibly sacred to Aly and me.

Cancer Free

We waited a week to find out the results of the breast tissue taken from Aly's mastectomy. Was there still cancer in the tissue they had removed even after chemotherapy? One of the positives about how our process unfolded is that due to Aly having chemotherapy before the mastectomy, it gave us a chance to find out if the chemo worked. Many people have chemotherapy after their mastectomy and never really know if the chemo did its job, so we were blessed by that, but obviously scared as well to find out the results.

As Dr. Litton (Aly's oncologist) came in our room, she said was bringing another doctor in with her. She brought him and began to talk. Aly and I just looked at her like, "Just tell us the results, and then we can small talk!" She proceeded to tell us that Aly was completely cancer free! There was no cancer in her tissue and no cancer in her lymph nodes. She was in shock, as this was not expected to happen.

We were in complete shock. We had hoped so much for this to happen but in the back of your mind you don't know if it was possible. We were told the week before that there was a 20% chance that Aly would be cancer free. Here she was beating statistics. All thanks and glory be to God, our Healer.

Chapter 5- Burden Carriers During the Journey

Importance of Mentors During Our Cancer Journey

When Aly was diagnosed, there was no one in my immediate family who could speak to what was about to take place. In the first month I went from being numb, to depressed, to guilty, to just plain confused. Early on in the process my dad and I were eating and he just looked at me and said, "Josh, there are not many things that will happen to you that I can't give wisdom or some advice, but this happens to be one thing that I truly have no experience with. Your mom never had breast cancer, and we certainly never had anything happen that was this serious as young as you guys are."

Some of our close friends have been through leukemia twice. They lost their grandfather and grandmother both to cancer. Richard and Angie have been through the crucible in a pretty astounding fashion. Angie was diagnosed with leukemia when I was about 12 years old. Then a few years later, she was diagnosed again. This time she was pregnant with their second child. We lived in the same neighborhood as Richard and Angie, and I remember my parents telling us what had happened, and we drove by their house. They were packing their car to head for treatment.

Angie delivered their beautiful daughter, Abigail and proceeded to beat leukemia again. Richard, her husband, had been through what I was about to go through. I had no idea when I was 12 as I watched them walk out their cancer journey, that this man would be such a vital mentor to me when my own wife was battling cancer.

In late November of 2011, I expressed to my dad that I felt like I was drowning. He thought I should go meet with Richard and see what he had to say. We met at a high-class joint called, Peking, a fancy chinese restaurant. Hopefully you can pick up on the sarcasm. I was able to share with Richard what I was feeling and thinking.

What was beginning to happen was an all out attack of Satan. When Aly was diagnosed, I was scared. Would she live? What would it look like? All kinds of thoughts flowed from that. Vain imaginations came in waves. You see when your wife is diagnosed with cancer you go to "What if she dies?"

Well the thought behind that is "What will I do?" That leads you to thinking about "Would I remarry?" That thought leads you to "Who would you look to marry?" In mere seconds you have a man that is completely broken by the idea of losing his wife to a man thinking about who he would marry if she died.

So quickly I went from a hurting man to an adulterer. I went from a loving husband to one who hoped his wife died.

Obviously I didn't really want Aly to die. In my mind though, there was an incredible battle underway. All the pressures of normal marriage and then stack on top of that the stresses of cancer, and I was combustible. As I shared some more detailed thoughts from depression to suicidal thoughts and everything in between, Richard said the words that let me off the hook. "Josh, you're not the only one." See the part that made the thoughts terrible was not just the thoughts, but the fact that I felt I was the only one that was having them. I believed the lie that I was too far gone to get help.

The struggle didn't stop after that conversation. I took drastic steps to guard myself from myself. Some of those were in my thought life but some of those were physical. I removed all guns from our house. I stopped doing anything that exposed me to failing. I quit playing golf. I couldn't handle failure. It took me to a place that was dangerous.

In that conversation and others, Richard gave me an understanding that for the road we were traveling these thoughts would be part of the fight. In the next chapter, I will talk about mentoring. What Richard did was mentor me. Mentoring is what happens when you turn around and help someone behind you come through the fire without as much damage.

A Passion For Mentoring Was Built

Richard mentoring me throughout our cancer journey birthed a passion inside of me to mentor others, as it had an extreme impact on me. If you can go through something and have someone impact you to an insurmountable level, and you don't feel the need to reach out to others, then I am not sure what that means about you. For me, I felt this huge urging by the Holy Spirit to do to others not only what was done for me, but to reach out even further to help men up the ladder that were behind me. Through this relationship with Richard and him mentoring me, I was given a clear example of what mentoring could do for someone.

I have had the opportunity to be mentored by some incredible people. When I was 19, I became of mentee of a man named Ron Scott. He is an incredible businessman, entrepreneur and Christian. Whether he knew it or not, he would alter the course of my life. I was exposed to real estate investment at 19, and I found a love for entrepreneurship.

I spent the next 18 months around Mr. Ron. He opened up a side of my personality that I honestly thought might be wrong. I am a dreamer, and he was too. Often times in our world, we are taught to take the safe route and doing things risky seem unwise, but I loved taking risks! He taught me and cultivated in me the desire and ability to see everything as an opportunity. I was groomed by a true entrepreneur, and to this day I have reaped the fruits of that.

Richard and Ron are just two mentors in my life. I have had others, but those two are at the top. As we made it through cancer, I knew it was my season to give back. If you find yourself wondering what you can do for someone and feeling at a loss, I encourage you to call up someone younger than you, invite them to coffee or lunch and ask if you can mentor them. They might look at you like you're crazy, but more often than not, people are begging for it, and wishing there was someone willing to pour into them.

As 2013 came around, I was in a different place and

God was continuing to heal me. I came across a website called: Radicalmentoring.com. It was started by a man named Regi, and what he and his team are doing is simply incredible. I knew that it was only by the grace of God that I was able to be the husband for Aly that she needed during her fight against cancer. But here's the thing: I wasn't ready. I had not adequately prepared myself. I simply was blessed to have some key people in my life that when the walls came down, they were ready to insert themselves to rebuild those walls, which would secure my success as a husband. Mentoring may have not only saved my wife's life, but mine as well.

Mentoring other men is all about the older generation connecting to the younger generation of men and not allowing them to fall in the same traps. I knew that I had to devote a huge part of my life to pouring into young guys, and that is exactly what I did and continue to strive to do.

When Richard reached out to me, he planted a seed. It was a seed that produced some quick fruit, but the real payoff came down the road. After time and just when I would need it, that seed bore fruit that changed my life. Because Richard had traveled the path I was going down, he knew what to speak to. Not just generalities. He knew exactly what would happen.

You see, Angie had been bald. Angie had been scared. Angie had fought for her life and needed to know her husband believed for her healing.

Had Richard not turned around and help me up the ladder, our story might look drastically different. Maybe I would have massively failed, but maybe not. What if I had just made it out? Or just gotten by? Here's the truth: That's not really living…just getting by. This mentor made this devastating time in my life and Aly's as a turning point for me in my relationship with God, and for that, I am forever grateful.

Here's the kicker. Richard was planting seeds for what would become the crucial moment for Josh Taylor. Little did I know that it would be what altered the trajectory of my life. It not only changed the trajectory of my life as a husband, but as a future father, and devoted follower of Christ. Mentoring matters. And God healed me through the mentoring of others.

Chapter 6 : Adoption Has Always Been A Dream

Adoption has always been interesting to me. At a young age I am sure I had no clue what exactly it was or what all went into it, but I do remember thinking I wanted to adopt. When you're young and think of adoption, you think of the cool things about another brother or sister. I thought about it from a sibling point of view when I was younger, and I just thought it was the neatest thing. I thought about the fact that if I could convince my mom and dad to adopt we would be that much closer to having our own basketball team. Picture of maturity, right?

So, yes much of my initial thoughts on adoption were that of a young kid, and maybe not the most rational (although a family basketball team would be legit). But none the less, I was interested. I thought about it a lot. The more I talk to people about adoption, I realize that the amount of time I spent thinking about it was out of the norm. That is now really amazing to look back on, because I can see God putting that desire in me as a little boy.

I grew up in a family with two kids. It was just my older brother Lee and I. Lee and I truly grew up together and were involved in seemingly every part of the others' life. I grew up having an incredible older brother who I wanted to be just like. Lee was the classic older child. He was far worse than I was with disobeying, but he was incredible at keeping his mouth shut longer than me (sneaky brother). I, however, was not as sneaky and was seen as a bit more of a trouble maker. I talked my way into most of my trouble. I did get to bask in the beauty of being the younger brother also, though. I developed much of my drive and personality from trying to keep up with Lee. I always looked up to my brother and still do. He is one of my best friends, even today.

I was always small and obviously younger than Lee and his friends, so I spent the majority of our growing up battling Lee and dad in sports around the house. Much of these times birthed my desire for another sibling because as a young guy I did not see the positive in always losing. I figured that if we could get another kid around the house my chances for winning went up drastically. Gosh, weren't my reasons for another brother or sister totally pure of heart? I wanted to save a child! Bring home a starving baby or a family who needed a home!

Okay, the reality as a little boy, was that I just wanted to win in sports against someone smaller than me. A perfect reason for adoption! I hope you are sensing the sarcasm here…

Growing up, my family and I spent the majority of our time around people. I also think this helped fuel the idea in my mind of the more people the better life would be. I always think "The more the merrier!" My wife, Aly, is much different than I. She would rather a small group of people to hang out with. My perspective is that more is more! Whoever came up with the "less is more" statement clearly didn't know what they were talking about.

If you can't tell yet as you are reading, I am very sarcastic, so if you think I am a careless, selfish, prideful man, well, yes, sometimes I am. But please read the sarcasm in this book. If you know me, you don't have to be told this, but for those of you thinking, "What in the world?", know that I really am a nice person (that's most likely up for debate☺).

Growing up, I really don't remember anyone I was around being adopted. The first person I really remember being around that was adopted was a friend in high school, and we played basketball together. Arthur was adopted by his family as an older child, and it all seemed cool from my perspective.

As we spent more time together through basketball it became clear even to a 17-year old that there are bumps in the road of adoption. I am sure there was much in the way of struggles that I didn't know or see, but to see a family take in a kid whose life would have been significantly different had they not taken and loved him as their own had a dramatic impact on my life.

There may be questions from the child who is adopted. There may be unasked questions from a teenager. I doubt there is a perfect adoption. Arthur's seemed to be a pretty good one though in my mind. That desire from a young boy wanting a basketball teammate began to grow into wanting to help a child have a forever family, not really knowing what that would look like down the road.

The only other time as a young kid that I remember anything about adoption was when my Aunt and Uncle adopted their son from Romania. They had been on mission trips, and had decided to adopt.

Their son, Josiah is now in his teens and is experiencing a life that I doubt he could have imagined in any other situation. I looked up to Uncle Bryan and Aunt Rhonda. I still do. Once again, this was another situation that birthed the desire in me to do this one day for another little one. Never doubt or look past things in your childhood or life that captured your heart or attention. God placed those desires and dreams in your heart for a reason. I do not like when people blow something off that was a passion of theirs when they were younger. God put that in them for a reason- seek out the why and see how God may want you to move forward with that passion.

Scared of Mission Trips

I am not sure when this first became a concern of mine but probably somewhere around 20 years old, I developed what I still consider to be a legitimate fear about mission trips. I was scared that if I went on a mission trip, I would come back with a child. I have a cousin who was adopted from Romania. I watched videos of orphanages, and if I saw that in person and came across children that were hurting, I really thought there would be no way I could leave without them. Sadly, that is still a main reason I haven't gone on a mission trip out of the country. How sad is that? But, I promised myself that when I wrote this book, I would be brutally honest with my readers, so that is what I am doing. I might be a terrible person for saying that, but honestly has to count for something, right?

Our church has supported a missionary family for as

long as I can remember. Inn Ministries in Guatemala was founded by Michael and LaTonya Lewis who now work at our church. I watched videos and heard stories my entire life of the amazing work that was going on at their church and school in Guatemala, and I was truly moved. I am still moved to this day when I hear stories of those children there. Aly and I sponsor a child there. Emilia is precious, and we treasure the notes she sends us.

I still never went to Guatemala. My entire family has gone except me. Aly wants to go with me, and I still say no. I just know that I can't take in a child right now, so I steer clear. This seems funny, but I am not joking. I literally thought that if I went on a mission trip I would not be able to turn down a need. If you know me, you know this is legitimate.

Please know, I can laugh at myself about this now. But it is all too true.

AAU Basketball

Growing up with my brother and dad, sports were a big deal to us. I don't mean that in a normal way, either. That was our hobby. We didn't hunt or fish like many boys and their dads did in the area we grew up. We watched and played sports together. Some of my fondest memories are at our first house on Briarcliff Drive with our basketball goal and batting cage. Aly will often talk about childhood movies and cartoons, and she is always baffled that I do not know about many shows. I try to explain to her that I was outside 24/7 playing some type of sport. TV was boring to me.

My dad had never played sports. If he had ever played football, I personally believe he would have been very good because of his drive and build. He quits for nothing. He loves everything about building teams and is fiercely competitive. I love that about my dad, and I am proud to say I got those good qualities from him.

Being the youngest and smallest in our family, meant I had to be tricky to have a chance in sports. Specifically when it comes to basketball, I had to learn to dribble and pass. In football, it meant I had to have an all out avoidance of contact. Seriously, have you seen me? Have you seen some of the big guys that play football? Yeah, avoidance of contact was key for Josh Taylor.

I may have been better at baseball, but basketball came the easiest for me. I truly loved the dynamics of basketball. I always played with older guys, and when I was older it developed me into a decent private school point guard. By no means a world changer, and I never hit the Rivals boards. But nonetheless, I was pretty good.

My gifts in basketball gave me an incredible opportunity after my junior year of high school to play on one of our states' top AAU basketball teams. This was the year after the team had gone to nationals, and this year was predicted to be the same. I remember the first practice I attended. Dad picked me up from my 99% white school, and we drove to the south side of Monroe, Louisiana. We walked into the back gym of Wossman high school in Monroe. Needless to say, I was out of my comfort zone. I walk in and Coach Foster from across the gym yells, "Midget, put your shoes on. Let's go!" I was hoping that was a term of endearment.

I slipped on my all white/ green Nike basketball shoes and walked out on the court with guys I had watched play in the big 5A city tournaments the year before. I had one thing on my mind and that was, "Don't do anything really stupid, Josh."

Coach Foster is an awesome man that runs the referee association in Monroe. He still does. That is how he found me. I had been around him quite a bit through recreational basketball leagues and then high school basketball, so I was semi comfortable with him. However, I was now on a basketball court with 9 of the most athletic guys I had ever seen, much less played against. To say their speed was on another level is an understatement. I don't recall doing anything grossly stupid that day, but I remember getting in the car and my dad just laughing.

These were my dad's first words as I got into the car, "Now that is basketball." Then he said some words that every kid needs to hear, "Josh, you can play basketball with those guys. You need this. Do you want to continue?" That was truly the first moment in my life that I was playing against and with guys that were far beyond my athletic ability. Sure, I could dribble a basketball, but these guys were out-of- the-box God-gifted athletes.

I ended up joining the team with the confidence from my dad, and it was some of the most fun I have had playing basketball. The more important thing that those 3 months showed me was how bad those other boys needed *their* dads. These are some of the most gifted athletes you will come across. One of the main athletes was insanely gifted. He was not there for our first practice but he came to a later practice and you would have thought Michael Jordan walked in. He was truly different. What I remember about him was not only his insane ability, but also the fact that he had a dad. Many of the guys did not have parents attend games. There were multiple games where the only parents in the stands were my dad and a family friend who is like a second dad to me, Martin West. I knew I mattered. Many of these kids simply did not know that, and that broke my 17-year-old heart.

After spending multiple weekends with this group of guys traveling our state, I came to an incredible realization. If they had my dad, their potential could have been realized. My dad isn't perfect, but he was present. Being present is huge, and most of these guys didn't have a dad that was present at all. This was a huge wake up call for me. Not only that these guys did not have present dads, but the kind of dad I wanted to be. Present, not perfect.

So many of these guys were incredible guys. But for so many of them the question is, what if?

What if they were born into my situation?

What if they were loved and pushed?

What if they knew they mattered?

This was another turning point for me where I was able to see how much these 17-18 year old guys loved to hang out with my dad and me. Not because we were that much fun, but because we were a family. They desired that, and they liked to be around that. I see that more even now in hindsight, but to see these talented athletes that looked like they could push me over with a simple nudge have an emptiness inside from not having a present father, and some even mothers, was something I had never experienced before.

One week, we were at a tournament in Baton Rouge, La, and had a break between games. One of the guys who became one of my better friends was named Chad. He was a 6' 5" wrecking ball left-hander from Carroll High School. There we were in a hotel room playing Madden on our X boxes while my dad napped. It hit me. There are so many kids that need this. They don't necessarily need lectures from a dad, but love. They don't need some pipe dream of a perfect family, but a mom and dad that say, "You matter."

You see, I had watched my parents love on people all my life. I knew people mattered. I knew I mattered.

I am not saying that these kids needs to be adopted, or that all of them weren't in good families. What I am saying is that I saw a group of guys that yearned for what my family gave me. This made me think of adoption and how the family people grow up in can truly change everything. I was getting one of my first pictures of why adoption can truly change someone's life. *It can change everything.*

Chapter Seven: When God Healed Me

As Aly went through cancer treatment, there were large amounts of attention given to what went on in her physically. What most people didn't realize is that there was something happening inside of *me*. God had used this process to start breaking away the things that didn't need to be a part of my life. Aly's battle was a physical one. There was obviously a huge spiritual element also. As Aly and I look back, we would be hard pressed to figure out who went through a bigger change. There is no doubt that Aly went through more, but who came out more changed? That is up for debate. The Josh that entered October 2011 when Aly was diagnosed with cancer was not a God-centered man. My identity was not in my relationship with God.

I had built a life and relationships on sand, unknowingly. That started to become increasingly more clear as the struggles seemed to keep on piling. Often times it is when the struggles keep piling when you realize what your life is truly built on.

The Conversation That Began Healing

Aly was diagnosed in October of 2011 and as of June 2012, I had still not completely surrendered to God. I had given him pieces and parts of my life throughout this tragedy, but I was holding on to one big piece. That big piece was money. I trusted God to heal my wife, but had not truly believed He would provide financially even though to that point He had done more than provide.

After Aly was diagnosed with breast cancer, I had gone and received my insurance license and was about to step into an already established business with a friend in the summer of 2012. I had kept this on the down-low during Aly's treatment. *Side note, anything that you hide is probably something you shouldn't do.*

I had not told my mentor, Richard, about this new venture that I had kept in my back pocket. It was in a sense a security blanket as I knew we were spending thousands of dollars on Aly's cancer treatments. One day during Aly's radiation treatment, we were headed to Houston for a visit in June when my phone rang. Richard was calling to 'check in.' Men that are mentoring and pouring into other men don't just 'check in.' Those kind of men call with a purpose. Those are the type men that you avoid when you think you may be doing something questionable and don't want to be called out. Well, that is how it is for me anyway. It isn't fun to have friends that give you constructive criticism. As I have learned, that is what good, Godly mentors do. They sometimes make you feel uncomfortable and ask hard questions to make sure you are following God with every part of your life. That is what I needed. That is what you need. That is what we all need!

Richard and I small-talked for a few minutes and then he said, "Josh, I hear you are starting in a new business? How is that going?" Insert: Crickets. He didn't badger me or lecture me. He spent the next few minutes speaking to what I had allowed God to do through me and that he believed in me. He mentioned that after our conversation just after Aly was diagnosed, he had seen me lay down what I needed to in order to be what Aly needed for me to be. He pointed out that God had blessed us in every way possible. Aly was healed. God had provided. In that moment what I came face to face with was that I was not trusting God with our money. He had already shown up and healed Aly. Yet I still thought I should trust *my* ability to provide over *His* ability. How ridiculous.

He was so right. I was depending on me when it had been proven that when I don't depend on myself, God comes through! I was broken. I wept and wept and wept in that car. How foolish?!? My miracle, my wife, was sitting next to me, and yet I thought I had a plan to control our money.

In that moment, God, through Richard, spoke to my heart. He called me to a higher level. One of the statements that has kept me from doing things that would deter me from following God's plan was this, "Josh, during this time in your life you need to be with Aly. She needs to have all of you. She needs to hear you believe she is healed. She needs to see she matters more than anything else. You WILL get past this, and in ten years you will wish you had let everything else go for this short time. Josh, you have succeeded up to now. Do not stop now. Love your wife with your time. Lay down your desires."

When I ended the phone call with Richard, I truly wept with Aly in the car. She just let me cry and was silent. When I settled down, she asked what happened, and I told her. From that moment on, I gave up the last piece I was holding on to. I committed to drop the last piece of an identity I held so dear. Money and financial planning had become an idol. It was where I found so much of my worth and identity. Me being an entrepreneur was no longer my identity. I then took an aggressive stance to distance myself from that. I knew at some point I could pick it back up, if and only if it had its' right standing in my life. Entrepreneurship would never be put before God and my trust in His ability to provide.

You see what just happened: That is mentoring. And to this day, I desire to mentor young men and help them know they are not alone and how abundant life can be when we give all of ourselves to an Almighty God that cares for us more than we can imagine.

I Started Living Differently.

Up until that point I took pride in having 10 different things going on at one time. I did real estate, I was the Director of Development at the school I worked for, I worked at used car lots, sold things on ebay, started businesses, and this list goes on and on. After that conversation in July of 2012 with Richard, I felt one thing from God. It was time to be broken. I had to be broken of everything that I had built to be important in my life. I went extreme. I cut off all real estate. I was not buying, selling, or building. My cousin and his wife were wanting to build a house at the time and after initial talks with them, I had to say I couldn't do it. In my mind I had let them down, and it killed me not to do it, because I wanted to! I had to have a conversation with my cousin and say that I couldn't build his house. I wasn't just letting him down, but he was letting his wife down. I was failing in my mind. Up until that point, I never said I couldn't or shouldn't do anything. I just did everything at 100 mph. In my mind, if you could, why wouldn't you? I learned to say no, as saying yes all the time really was saying no to many things that truly mattered.

When I finally started saying no to things, what I was actually doing was saying out loud to men that "I wasn't enough." I didn't have enough emotional, spiritual, and physical energy to build my cousin's house, while at the same time honoring what God wanted me to do. I didn't know how long this would last, but I heard clearly that I was to tell people I am no longer an entrepreneur. That broke my business heart because that is what I was known as. It was so clear that had become my identity. I had to go that extreme to allow God to truly break me and my shallowness.

I was not sure when I would be able to pick those things back up that I loved so much, but I knew beyond a shadow of a doubt that I was supposed to lay that piece of me down for this time until I was able to do it with its right place in my life. I became Josh Taylor, Director of Development at Claiborne Christian School. And better than that, I just wanted to be known as Josh Taylor, child of God. Husband to Aly. I wanted to get to the place where people weren't even sure what I did for a living, because that was simply not the most important part of me. I committed to doing nothing else outside of my main job as Director of Development. Nothing else. Not what I would say was flashy or impressive. Little did I know it was God laying the groundwork for my brokenness. In order to be healed, I had to be broken, and oh- I needed to be healed more than I ever realized!

Another thing Richard said was that I should pray that God would cut open my heart and lay it flat and examine it. I need to ask Him to reveal the darkness I had allowed inside. I needed to pray for God to reveal everything that I had allowed to take residence in my heart that was evil. And I then needed to pray that God would replace all the evil with his Holy Spirit, and that I would be what God had called me to be. It became my prayer. It became my mantra. Daily.

Ask for brokenness, and let me tell you, you will get it. What ended up happening was a complete change. In the last few groups I have shared my story with, I have been asked how I knew it was okay to start being an entrepreneur again. The answer to that question literally gives me chills each time I say it.

I believe God's time-table for me to return to entrepreneurial action was based on my heart change. Somewhere along the way I no longer found my identity in what I did as an entrepreneur. I found my identity in what God was making me. I truly didn't think about businesses. I thought about God. I don't mean to make that too spiritual, but it's just the truth.

Little by little, I believe God has turned the flow back on. That flow at this point is far beyond what it ever was before I surrendered to God's will for me. That isn't just fun-talk. That is quantifiable, and I can show that to be true. God is faithful.

I prayed for brokenness for a calendar year. God has shown up again in ways I could never deserve. Being broken truly sets you up to be healed and whole.

Steps I Took to Change

When I think about the literal steps I took toward change, they are simple. They were not so simple when I was in the middle of the process though. If you are like me, you read a book like this and think, "I want steps!" Well, here is what I did in hopes of helping you with whatever is holding you back from being completely broken before God.

- I stopped cold-turkey telling people I was an entrepreneur. In multiple situations I was offered to buy or build a house, and I gave that opportunity up. I told people I wasn't doing that anymore. I asked God to break me of me.

- Every thought I had that I thought was not of God, I would say out loud, "Satan there is no room for you here."

- I told other men in my life of my intentions. I then told them that if they saw me waver, that they were to question me. That is what true friendship is all about- not allowing your friend to make decisions that pull them away from Jesus, and I was upfront with my friends about needing their help. I couldn't do it alone.

Chapter Eight: Starting Where the Journey Began: Baby-Making

Dr. says "Okay" to Begin Attempting Pregnancy Again

In October of 2011, we were looking forward to starting our family. Learning Aly had breast cancer was a double whammy because not only was her life at stake, but when you are trying to get pregnant and find out you have cancer, you pray you will have children, but our main focus was on saving Aly's life. We were even scared that when Aly was diagnosed with breast cancer that she was pregnant. We realized her not getting pregnant quickly was a blessing, because it would have been a completely different road had she been pregnant when she was diagnosed. Had she gotten pregnant, I don't even want to think about all of the decisions we would have had to make regarding Aly's treatment. But regardless, attempting pregnancy is what led Aly to find her breast lump. For that, we are grateful. That is where all of this started. This crazy journey. It all started with attempting pregnancy.

Then October 2013 came around, and we were headed to see Aly's oncologist, Dr. Litton. This is the meeting we marked on our calendar years ago. The day we would pick up where we left off. You see, we were told to wait for 2 years from Aly's breast cancer diagnosis to attempt pregnancy again. The type of breast cancer she had was very likely to recur in the first two years following her diagnosis, and of course they did not want her to get pregnant during those years, so you better believe we had been counting down to that two year mark, for many reasons! It meant Aly's cancer had not recurred, and we could start trying again to grow our family.

This day on our 2 year mark, we would get released to attempt trying to have a child. For us, this day could not come fast enough for multiple reasons. I know that as Aly underwent treatment there were many days we talked about not knowing if we would have children. This day was the day we would receive the "go ahead" to again head that way. Days like this serve as another check-point in healing. When the doctor looked at Aly and says yes or no to having a baby, it gave us another mark on the path. We needed hope.

As we headed to Houston, we expected good news. So many trips we spent going to Houston didn't have hope attached to them. We had made more than 90 round trips to Houston at that point. The trip was 6 hours there and 6 hours back. Not many of those trips were carrying the potential for good news like this one.

We were sitting in the waiting room where all this started almost 2 years ago. Unbelievable. Those are the moments I had no clue would come. When I would be able to look at treatment in the distance. An opportunity to say "remember when?" Those moments feel like they will never come. There is nothing more rewarding than looking in the rear view mirror remembering what God has brought you through, rather than walking in it.

Aly and I were sitting in the doctor's room just waiting for her doctor to walk in. When she did walk in and asked the normal questions, we were both listening for one sentence. We both admitted to not hearing or remembering much else from the meeting. We heard what we were desperate to hear.

Dr. Litton said that we could begin attempting pregnancy again! Aly's scans came back clear and was in good health. I knew this was good news. As I would come to find out though, getting to try and have a baby brings all new things into your life.

Baby-Making

Life was about to get good, right? What is better for a

29 year-old than having a wife that is desperate to get pregnant? This means all we will do is have sex right? You know, this is what I waited for my wedding night to do, so it was party time! Well, let me just say that I had a bit of an education headed my way. I never knew there were calendars for this stuff. Certain temperatures. I will not go into too much detail but suffice it to say that I think this should be called "baby planning", not "baby-making." This was not what I expected.

Our lives began to revolve around ovulation and a test that told us the right "time" to engage in sexual relations. When that little tester showed a smiley face, my world stopped until we had "addressed the situation". Anything on-demand makes that process more interesting. I quickly learned that this process of baby-making was much more difficult than I thought. It wouldn't be all fun and games, especially when there was so much emotion and anticipation of it all.

However, when you're called upon on certain days at certain times because a tester said it was "go time", the whole process is thrown into a twist. This process in no way made me dislike my wife sexually. It did however create some interesting conversations and situations to say the least!

The funniest example from this part of our life was when I broke my nose. I have played sports my entire life and never broken a bone. I don't know that I have even had a serious sprain. Outside of a jammed finger, I had escaped my childhood and adolescence completely pain free. That is a miracle in and of itself counting all of the crazy things I did growing up.

That all came to an end in April of 2014 in a recreation league basketball game. One of the most fun times of the year for me is getting to play recreational basketball with the boys from Claiborne Christian School. Any of the guys that do not play baseball were offered the opportunity to play some off-season basketball with me. Kyle Walker, Cory Walker, William Fulton and some other CCS Alums or supporters would also play with us. Our team name is the Laird Street Stampede. Quite a force to be reckoned with. Sounds intimidating, right? Be afraid, be very afraid.

In our 2nd game of the year, I was running with the ball full speed down the right side of the floor. We had just rebounded the ball on defense, and were fast breaking. Just about the time I crossed half court, a guy cut in front of me. At that point I had the idea of a 17 year-old and put the ball behind my back. I can still do this, right? Oh yeah.

Up until that point, my 29-year-old body was responding okay. Somewhere between everything going okay and about to go really bad, my body couldn't keep up. The ball came from behind my back and bounced a little too far out in front of me. When it did, I turned left and leaned forward to catch back up and the next thing I knew, I woke up and was laying on the ground with blood on my face. I had turned directly into the shoulder of a guy that was running full speed the opposite direction.

I had shattered my nose. I hoped it was just a good hit, but when we arrived home that night, I knew something was bad wrong. The doctor confirmed it later the next day. It was broken in several places.

I ended up having surgery the next week. Just to let you know, I am a hypochondriac. I am also scared of doctors of any kind. I think I held up okay for the most part right until surgery time. I was telling Aly that my Dad would take care of her and that I loved her in case something happened during surgery. You would have thought I was having open heart surgery. Pretty ridiculous stuff. But that is the truth. I was convinced that the sleep medicine would take me out for good. Now you know something embarrassing about me. Congrats.

I had my nose surgery and started recuperating at home. There is also a funny story where I had a panic attack the day after my surgery and thought I was having a heart attack. I couldn't breathe. We went to the emergency room and had to get some sedative. It was ruled that I was simply having a panic attack. That glorious shot did the trick. Mind you all, this manliness happened to a guy who is married to Aly Taylor, "captain no pain".

A few days after my nose surgery, Aly took one of those pee strip tests (yes I know there is a better, more professional name for those things), and it told her she was ovulating. I was so incredibly doped up on pain medicine sleeping in our living room, and in comes a lady on a mission. Let's just say attempting making a baby did not happen that night. It ended with Aly in tears. I learned that hydrocodone and attempting to make a baby don't mix. I think you can fill in the blanks here!

Each Month Was a Roller Coaster

As we started walking down the road to pregnancy, it became clear that this was an "all or nothing" thing. I know that sounds like a rather obvious statement, but here's what I mean. For 25 days of the month, everything was good. We were following all the schedules and doing what we were supposed to do, which created hope.

Then in the blink of an eye when Aly would test herself and find out that she was not pregnant, we were back in the figurative basement. This is one of the situations where our history made each failed pregnancy test hurt worse. Each month that came back negative made Aly re-approach the idea of cancer and what it had possibly done to her. What it had possibly taken from her. What it had taken from us.

I obviously know some of what Aly has gone through because she had voiced those hurts each month. On the flip side I know there are quite many more hurts she was not saying. As a husband I often wondered, "What do I do?" I was constantly going back and forth between hope and hurt. Should I continue to stay positive and could possibly set my wife up for heartbreak, or should I begin preparing our hearts for what could be possible- that we wouldn't make a baby.

As I would talk to a few of my friends who would ask how that month was, all I could tell them was it seemed as we were either on the mountain top or in the gutter. I don't remember very many just "normal" days, whatever those are. So many of them were spent in hope or hurt. Trying to find a solution.

It didn't help that during Aly's diagnosis and treatment it seemed as if every one of our friends had babies. Literally everyone we know got pregnant in the last 3 years. Okay, maybe a bit of an over exaggeration, but not by much. Needless to say, that was not always easy.

Others' Pregnancy Announcements

Aly and I were living in Houston in the summer of 2012 when the flood started. No, not a literal flood, but one that seemed worse than that. As we were tackling radiation treatment and as I saw my wife's skin have burns on it as if she was in a literal fire, others' lives kept going on. Yes, I know life does that, but it was hard to see that while our world had stopped, and we were fighting for my wife's life, that others seemed to be living worry-free lives, while experiencing many joyous occasions. I was jealous. At times I was angry.

During Aly's radiation treatment, we received a call from my brother and his wife. They proceeded to tell us they were pregnant! When we tell you we were excited for them, we mean that with our whole hearts. That is not fake. Our hurt was very real also though.

I would be lying if I said that there were not moments of

extreme hurt and at my core a desire to get away from the talk of pregnancy. I wanted my parents to celebrate with my brother and his wife, but on the other hand, I wanted them to be hurt for us. I can only imagine what it was like for my brother and his wife to have to tell us the news. To talk about it in front of us. They knew we were happy for them, but that we wanted that to be our story too. We wanted to be celebrating. Our life had stopped in its tracks. Their life was taking off. And we made it a point to tell them and others that we were happy for them, and we did not want it to be awkward for them to talk about their pregnancy in front of us. We meant that, but that does not mean it was any less difficult.

What a quandary. I had to ask myself, "Are you going to be a jerk or choose happiness and love?" I was crazy happy but my heart was hurt. I wanted to be a dad. I wanted to have the first grand kid. That's just the truth. All in all I think that my family did an incredible job of trying to be balanced.

There is no perfect way for this process to go down. You just commit to love like crazy and be honest about the hurt.

Chapter Nine: Yet Another Diagnosis

We Learn the Severity of Aly's Infertility

At some point in the process of trying to get pregnant the fear comes in. "Can we get pregnant?" In any case it is my understanding that women begin to worry pretty quickly. Add to that the fact of what we had been through and it did not take long for us to start to look for more options. We had wanted to become parents for years, so once we got the "okay" to begin trying again, we were ready, and I mean ready!

This led us to research fertility doctors. When I say us, I mean Aly. I was certainly concerned, but to be honest I would have kept going and just hoped it would have worked. In our situation though we had been warned this could be a possibility. We ended up going to a doctor in Mississippi that had helped one of Aly's friends get pregnant. We were referred to a fertility specialist after being on fertility medications with no success.

As we sat and talked with the fertility specialist, he told us all about the process of IVF and other treatments. It was decided on that first visit that we would try a drug called

Femara first. This was done in hopes that it would kick Aly's ovaries into overdrive and help her produce more eggs. We did this the first month after being referred to the fertility specialist.

I can honestly say during this part of the process there was no big change for me. I still believed that this medicine would help, and we would be able to have a baby. We agreed that we would go the first month and when Aly ovulated, the doctor would test it, and we would find out how her egg production was.

As we headed home from that first visit I wasn't sure what to think. I can tell you I just hoped it worked. I didn't want Aly to have to face anything else. That was for the most part my only thoughts. I didn't want to see my wife hurt again.

IVF?

After the first month of the Femara medication, we were certainly hopeful. Aly had shown on an ovulation kit that the time was right, so we did everything we could to make it happen (this time no nose surgery got in the way ☺). As we headed back to Mississippi to meet with the doctor, I remember simply hoping the numbers were good. I simply hoped that it showed Aly had a great ovulation.

Whether or not we were pregnant was secondary to me at that point. If the test came back that Aly had ovulated well and produced plenty of eggs, then I assumed we would just trudge on with the medicine. We went in the doctor's office truly hopeful.

As we sat and talked to the doctor, we found out that it had not been great. We found out that he thought we should go to IVF- immediately. I had no clue what IVF was other than to say that a baby would be formed in a dish, and I was against that. As I heard him talk about it, I didn't know what to think. As he talked everything involved, it became crystal clear just how advanced medicine is. Doctors can literally do anything we can imagine. He explained that Aly's egg quality and quantity were extremely low. He said she was in pre-menopause. If she would ever get pregnant, her best bet would be by IVF, and because she was in pre-menopause, we needed to do IVF immediately if we felt comfortable with it.

We left his office that day agreeing to jump in the next group to do IVF at their clinic. We decided if that however many babies were created that we would implant each one. We could never, ever "discard" a baby. We knew that might mean lots of babies, but when your fertility is compromised, we both thought, "We will take whatever God gives us!"

IVF is not cheap. IVF is controversial.

I knew this and as far as the money goes, I was just believing it would be okay. We ended up taking some of our savings and paying for the IVF. As a husband, this was one of those moments where I felt the intense need to let Aly know this wasn't about money. If that meant I had to sell stuff, then so be it. We were going to go down this road. We never wanted money to be a hindrance to us doing something we felt God leading us to. We had to trust that God would provide.

Where IVF stood out as much different than cancer treatment was its finality. With cancer treatment, it was a bit unending. When you look at IVF, you will see that you get a very clear answer. It either works or it doesn't. Knowing that the step after IVF was egg donation or adoption helped me decide on doing IVF. I wanted to make sure that wherever we ended up that I could look at Aly and say, "We did everything in our power to make it happen." And we wanted to be sure we were following God's leading. We knew if we couldn't get pregnant, it would be a clear way of God leading us to have children through another avenue.

Babies being in created in a dish is controversial. This

was on my mind immediately. I will not sell myself as an authority on this subject, but I will tell you how I made the decision that we were cool with, and how we did the process.

I gave Aly shots for about 3 weeks. When she began to ovulate (release eggs), we called the doctor. The doctor then removed what fluid he could from Aly's ovaries. In that fluid were the eggs that she had produced. Those eggs were then combined with my sperm to create an embryo. Every egg and sperm either succeeds or fails. If they become an embyo (a baby in our mind), then you have options.

This is where science can be amazing or devastating.

You have the option to have the embryos tested. You can find out everything you could want to know plus some you don't about an embryo. You will then be presented by your doctor the option to implant, hold, donate or discard.

*At this point we are considering embryos = babies. I am just using that word for the scientific part of the explanation.

Now, that is the nuts and bolts of the process. Not our process but that is the quick version. Now for our story and what we decided.

When we left the doctor's office after the first visit, Aly

and I had discussed this. So now after our second visit we already knew what we were doing. I made one promise to Aly. We discussed that if we ended up at IVF, there were a few things we would not consider.

We decided to not get our embryos tested. This in my opinion was useless to us because we would not be acting any differently no matter what the doctor told us about the embryo. In our world that was a baby. Period. We decided we would never discard an embryo- whether it showed an abnormality or would most likely result in miscarriage. We would give each baby a chance.

So why would we have them test the embryo to tell us what's wrong? We were believing just like any other set of parents that our baby would be exactly what God had planned for it. I like to make my decision in situations like this before we get there. This takes the emotion out of it.

It is much the same as setting a price before you enter to buy a car--- Anything over that and you walk. Same thing for us. It didn't matter.

Back to Aly. So in our situation we were able to get two eggs from Aly. For us that was a miracle. Those two eggs were combined with my sperm in the lab. We would then know in a few days if they survived or not. This was a complete miracle, as the fertility doctor told us to discontinue our IVF in the middle of treatment because he felt like he would not be able to retrieve any eggs. We decided to continue on, in faith. We were used to bad statistics and believing against our "odds".

We found out that both embryos made it to day 3! When we went in on day 5 to get them implanted into Aly, the doctor had devastating news for us. One of the embryos in his words did not continue growing. To which I immediately made him clarify that he was not making a decision for us. I wanted to hear him say that the embryo had ceased growing.

He was able to show us on a chart where our good embryo had multiplied cells drastically. The other embryo after day 4 had stopped growing. It expired. This was super important to us to let them understand that if there was a functioning embryo that it was to be put inside Aly. Our decision for implantation happened when sperm met egg. Period.

The only other option for us would have been embryo donation. If Aly had produced 20 eggs and those 20 eggs were viable and good then we would have been beyond happy to donate them to someone who needed them. We did know going in however that there was a very low chance of this because of the doctor being discouraged that we would get any eggs at all.

Was I Thinking About Adopting During IVF?

Our family was at lunch at Logan's as we told them about our decision to do IVF. I followed that up with one order. We would not discuss egg donation, adoption, surrogacy or any other plan of having a child. To discuss any of those options felt like I was giving up on God doing a miracle through and in Aly. I had a clear understanding that without God deciding to make a baby happen by our genetics, that most likely adoption or another option would be the route we would take.

I just wanted Aly to know I was fighting and believing that she would give birth to a child. I wanted to believe it wholeheartedly also. I am not sure if this was self-protection or just stubbornness. As I told you all throughout Aly's cancer journey, I always had a "back up plan." What that back up plan did was squash my faith. I was choosing to believe. And if conceiving a baby was not God's will for Aly and me, then we would put our faith in something else. But for the moment, I had to believe that we would conceive and bear a child.

Our Failed IVF

IVF was an incredible process. I gave Aly 2 or more shots each day when we were going through the process. Her belly looked like a war zone. I administered the shots all around her belly button. It looked terrible with all different colored bruises.

We ended up having one viable embryo to implant in Aly. What an incredible process! I was able to be in the room as the doctor inserted our baby into Aly's uterus. I watched through an ultrasound screen as the tube went toward the uterus and then as the baby slid down the tube into Aly.

What an incredible thing that men have figured out how to make this happen with such precision. We left that day with our spirits so high. We truly believed Aly would become pregnant, and we would have a baby in our arms so soon. As the next days went on, we just couldn't wait to hear that we were pregnant. This was a long time coming.

At this point, we were almost 3 years since we had started trying. This was mid-August 2014. Many people are willing to let you see their high points. Few people are willing to let you see heartbreak. On the day we knew the doctor was going to call my wife to tell us if we were pregnant or not, we set up a video camera. We wanted to get our reactions as we found out we would be parents. As the phone rang, we sat down and she took the call. Our hearts were beating out of our chests.

I sat there as Aly answered the phone with a huge smile on her face, and then I saw the look I had become accustomed to. Devastation and disappointment. Very quickly, we found out that we were not pregnant. Heartbreak. This is the day we had hoped for, the day we would get the results, but certainly not the outcome. We had visions and plans of how we would tell our parents. Aly was certainly broken in this moment. I remember hurting, but was cool with the fact that we had done everything we could to make it happen. There was nothing more we could test. Nothing more we could do. Had we stopped mid-IVF as our doctor suggested, I think we may have wondered, "What if we kept going?" "What if we would have allowed God to do a miracle?" We now knew that it was not His will for us to get pregnant through this fertility treatment.

Devastation to Hope to Devastation to Hope

I was so tired of the up and down. That wasn't okay with me. I remember back during 2012 when Aly had to have emergency reconstructive surgery because the skin on her breast had failed. I was working on a deer stand in July, and my friend Jason called because he heard we were going to Houston the next day. I remember telling him I was tired of seeing Aly hurt.

It seemed to be unending. This kind of qualified. I was frustrated. I was tired of consoling her. I wanted to party with her. I wanted to celebrate. I frankly had enough of the whole "let down" phase of our life. This part of the journey was especially rough because we were elated to retrieve eggs. We were then blown away that both eggs had turned to embryos. It was as if the momentum was building for a huge miracle- a pregnancy, a baby. And then after that momentum and hope came the news that she was not pregnant.

Frankly I was tired of the gutter. The gutter is never a good place to find yourself. We all want to experience the moments of victory, not the gutter moments. I was so sick of the gutter. Apparently, God was teaching us how to not only survive the gutter, but enjoy life in the gutter.

Did you know that? That we can actually *enjoy* life when it is less than peachy? I actually think that God can give an extra level of love and grace in the gutter if we allow Him to.

Chapter 10: Adoption Wasn't Second Best

When we came off of the news of our failed IVF treatment, we decided to not tell anyone for a while. There have been things we have done in our process that I am not sure I would do again like we did them. This was not one of those items. This time where only we knew that we had not gotten pregnant gave us the chance to mourn this process. It was literal mourning. We did not know what to do. We spent time on our face before God. Similar as when we found out Aly had cancer, there was an unspoken connectedness between Aly and me. But we were left with so many questions.

Were we supposed to try IVF again? Should we just continue attempting pregnancy on our own? Should we find an egg donor, like our fertility doctor suggested? Should we adopt?

We didn't look at adoption as a bad thing or second best. It simply wasn't where we had started. I remember the day that now Aly says she realized we were ready to adopt. I was in my office working, and she walked in. She proceeded to tell me about what seemed to be an incredible opportunity to adopt a baby in Alabama.

It was an incredible opportunity. It was a young girl who just wasn't yet ready to be a mom. Aly told me to think about it, but I immediately said yes. I think it was in that moment that our heart was shown. We didn't look at adoption as a backup plan. It just simply wasn't the plan we thought God had for us. Oh, how we had no clue! We were excited about the possibility of this situation.

I had struggled with the idea of adoption for the most part from the point that it felt like we were quitting on God. I know that we were not literally quitting, but to a degree it made me feel that way. When Aly's oncologist told us that we did not have time to preserve her fertility, we so deeply believed that God would protect Aly's womb and that she would become pregnant. It wasn't that we wanted a biological baby so greatly, as much as it was we felt like we did not believe anymore what we believed with much conviction when Aly was undergoing her cancer treatment. In reality we weren't going to stop trying for a baby. What we were agreeing to was to start the process of seeing if God had a baby that needed us. Adoption and its process was the start of us completely surrendering to God. Saying we've done all we know to do, and now it is in your hands. In retrospect, I know God was wanting this from us the whole time. We humans can make things so difficult.

Adoption is Overwhelming

Adoption is overwhelming. So many different options. What country would we adopt from? What criteria would we say we were looking for? Race? Drug abuse? Disabilities? The options when you go down the adoption road are truly endless. We were unsure on so many things, but we started feeling like we were to go through with a domestic adoption. Maybe down the road God would have us adopt internationally, but for now, we both felt like domestic adoption was where we would start, and we would need God to direct us with all of the other options, as we were clueless and overwhelmed.

As I have said in other parts of this book, my wife is a researcher. There are both positives and negatives to this talent. The good is that you know everything that is available. The bad is that you know everything that is available. Once your heart is turned toward adoption you see all the need. There are literally thousands upon thousands of orphans. We wanted them all. At the time of starting the adoption process, we were living in a one-bedroom apartment. This desire for us was growing, but we were clueless of how it would all go down.

For us, a new battle was brewing. What would we do? Where would we go to adopt?

There are international adoptions. You go through a big agency. You tell them where you want to adopt from, and they take it from there. It seemed to me to be a pretty sterile process. I have a cousin who was born in Romania. I believe in this type of adoption. I simply didn't know what route we would end up taking.

I knew adoption was expensive. Very expensive. We had committed early on that money would not play a part in our deciding what type of adoption we would pursue. I would be naive to say that it never crossed my mind though. Someone told Aly early on a phrase that has stuck with us. They said, "God funds what He favors." We believed that. We knew God favored adoption. After all, He adopted us. Therefore, we trusted Him wholeheartedly with the finances.

The next kind of adoption that Aly told me about was a US agency where we would look to adopt a US baby. This, too, seemed pretty sterile. Submit the paperwork, and hope to be picked. There was nothing overtly negative in my mind about this route, and honestly I thought this is where we would end up. There was a consultant agency and an attorney in town, and these two options became the ones that seemed to be what we felt like we would do to bring home Baby Taylor.

The only other option we came across was through my childhood babysitter. She and her husband had adopted through an attorney in Florida and loved it. They spoke highly about the system. As Aly researched and watched what this attorney did, we became comfortable with his system. It was much different than a typical adoption agency, but it made it very risky as well.

We were able to see success rates. We were able to watch other people enter the process. His process was anything but sterile. We would be able to watch as opportunities came up, and if we were interested we could apply. He would send out emails as birth mothers came to him and then couples would apply for that case. Then, the birth mother and/or birth father would choose the adoptive parents of the baby.
But then came my concern.

Are we buying a baby? I probably should have had this worry sooner, but in essence I felt like maybe we were supposed to just put our name in a hat and not let any of our attributes help us. Were we supposed to just start living and believe that since our hearts were open to adoption that God would give opportunities?

What helped me get past this was the process of the attorney we went with. None of the money we were paying was profit to the birth mom in my mind. It went to cover attorney fees, which we could see detailed. It went to cover the cost of the birth mother's pregnancy. That means everything about their pregnancy. That means the health of the baby. That helped me mentally, but the price of adoption still makes me angry when I think about it.

Are We Hearing God?

So much of this part of our journey was spent trying to make sure we were hearing from God and not acting out of hurt. We wanted to make sure that we weren't going ditch to ditch in an effort to become parents. I think one of the most common questions we are asked is "How did we know what to do?" That has been in reference to business deals all the way to cancer treatment.

What our answer is every time is the same. We hold firm to the belief that God grants wisdom. In the absence of

God writing on our wall, we depend on his wisdom. Some times I think people look at us and wonder how we know what to do. My answer is "We don't." We simply believe the Holy Spirit is working within us, and as we ask for guidance and wisdom, He gives that to us. Really throughout our entire journey, outside of the end of our adoption story, there were no "wall writing" moments. Simply trusting and forging ahead. Trusting that God was guiding our every step.

We do however wake up everyday and try and stay directly in line with the will of God for our lives. I have believed that in simple things like buying trucks, and I have believed that in picking cancer treatments. Mine and Aly's wisdom is simply not enough. When we have found ourselves outside of God's will it is because we missed him. We either didn't hear or didn't wait, or weren't seeking His guidance.

I do however prefer to fail moving forward. If I make a mistake, it will most likely be due to aggression. I don't ever want to be in opposition of Proverbs where I move to quickly and don't seek wise counsel. Once you do seek wise counsel and feel as though you have all the good information you can gather, you must forge ahead. Joyce Meyer once said, "You can't move a parked car. In order for God to direct you, you have to be moving."

This is what I said to Aly as we contemplated what route to take toward adoption. She asked "What should we do?" My only answer is keep forging ahead. It is far easier to steer a moving ship. Period.

With that said, we moved forward with our home study. Not because we knew that was the thing to do but because almost every opportunity we could apply for was going to require a home study. So what if we had decided to go a route that didn't require that? Well, so what. We did what we could do and started getting a home study. We had no idea how these little decisions would be lining us up for our baby.

Chapter 11: The Calls

We made the decision to go ahead with the home study. This gave us the option to apply to almost any agency in the world. Once we had this, there was no baby that could come up that we couldn't have join our family if the birth parents consented. For us, this was the first real step toward being legitimate parents.

As a matter of fact this was the first time someone else called us "parents". The social worker conducting the home study kept referring to us as parents and one day when she left, Aly pointed that out through tears. We were parents. Most likely at that point our baby was already conceived. There was a legitimate chance baby Taylor was alive and kicking somebody. Hopefully with a right foot.

It was a Friday when we received the email that there was a baby in Florida that Aly had a feeling about. Aly and I were both very excited. All we had to do to apply was fill out a form and send in a little money and we were considered applicants.

We were pumped. Not because we were guaranteed

anything but because the Taylor gang was getting closer to becoming 3 than ever before. That for us was fun. It was about 2 hours later after Aly and I received the info of the baby in Florida that Aly's phone rang. She looked at the caller ID and told me that it was a lady in south Louisiana from an adoption agency who had been given our name by a friend.

She also had an opportunity for us. The difference with this case was that there was….get ready for it….TWINS. For me it seemed like a no brainer. We can handle twins. To be honest I didn't know if we could handle one. I do have a theory though that has proved true in most pools. Anything over 5'3" is above my nose which means I'm swimming. So you can't scare me with a 20' ft deep pool. It's all the same once I'm swimming.

Children surely worked the same, right? I mean Aly could handle that couldn't she? Because I just planned on having fun with the children anyway. She does the work and I am there for fun. I can see Aly's face as I say this now! Aly reminded me that during our home study the social worker asked me what I thought would be different once we had a child. My answer was "Not much." I told her I would bring the kids with me or Aly could take care of them. Seems pretty straight forward, huh? Little did I know my wife was eavesdropping on that conversation, so we had a good laugh later.

I love opportunity. I do not like feeling like I have no options. So of course my idea was to apply for both situations and just believe again that God would show up and make it clear which one we should go for. One important piece of information that makes our story so crazy also. The twins only had 3 applicants. The baby in Florida had 22 applicants. We were told there was a really high chance we would be chosen for the twin case, as the birth mother was looking for parents like us, but our hopes weren't as high with the case in Florida with the 22 applicants.

Up to this point in our adoption journey, I honestly had hoped that we could go through this process without anyone knowing it. That way if we were let down at some point I didn't have to be consoled. I am not sure why, but I do not like that. I don't like being felt sorry for, and I have a hard time naturally letting people help me.

I remember being in the woods in a deer stand and hearing God tell me that Aly needed to *experience pregnancy*. Not necessarily a physical pregnancy, but a spiritual and emotional pregnancy. The celebration of a life to come. Because I was guarding against hurt, I was also stripping her from the ability to be "pregnant", even if that meant an "adoption pregnancy."

I walked in the apartment to tell her what I felt God tell me to say to her, and before I could, I could tell something happened. She was literally giddy. Like make me want to hurt someone giddy. I don't know why I get aggravated when people seem excited. It's probably something totally horrible about myself, but it's true. When I don't understand someone's excitement, I can get super irritable. Regardless, I sat her down on the couch and proceeded to tell her that I wanted to celebrate this adoption journey, this adoption pregnancy. I understood that this would be a key part to this for her.

I believe that now more than ever. Women are a truly special breed, and there are some things no matter what, the risks are worth it. After tears and me sharing that with her, she shared with me the adoption situation in Florida and that she just had a "feeling" about it. It was as if I had finally given her a reason to be excited, instead of her feeling like we couldn't talk about it or get our hopes up.

At that point, my emotions about applying for these two

cases were somewhat mixed. I understood we may not get selected. I also understood on paper that we are not the "typical" couple looking to adopt. We are super young. But we are seemingly stable and anxious to provide love and life to a child that needs it. I knew that if I was a birth parent looking for someone to take the child I created, I would want a couple like us! Yes, I like me some me. So, I knew there were lots of chances we wouldn't get chosen, but I also thought we had a good chance of being chosen too, which made me excited, but scared all at the same time.

In the end, Aly and I agreed we would submit for both situations. We simply prayed that God would show us what to do. Now for the real world thought behind applying for both situations

First, the law of percentages would tell you the more you apply for, the higher your chances are. We felt that both situations were suitable for us. Therefore we made the decision to move on with both. So what would we have done if both had chosen us? We would have gone and visited with both birth moms. Why? Because just as with any adoption, something could happen in either case. And we would trust the Lord to guide us of who we would be matched with. In our world options are everything. And by options I don't just mean options in the way of "security nets" but moreso leaving room for God to direct us. Remember the moving ship reference I discussed earlier? We just kept moving and praying for direction. How were we supposed to choose over either case?! And of course we also knew there would be a chance we would end up with 3 babies. That would be crazy, but if that were to happen, we knew God would give us the grace to do it.

This was a prime example of forging ahead in my mind. We did not need to make any definite decisions. We still had time for there to be writing on the wall. By keeping our names in the hat, we were also allowing God to move in those situations. Sometimes I think we as Christians get stuck on tangibly hearing words from God on direction. My argument would be that we should act in belief that God is going to move.

But don't get me wrong here. We weren't just jumping in. We had weighed the situations. We sought wisdom. We were going to move both situations forward and let God act inside of them. All the while, we were still seeking to hear from God. I promise at any point we would have been glad for God to speak directly to us! We just hadn't heard that yet and kept forging forward.

Once we decided to apply for both situations, I went through all kinds of thoughts. My natural bent is to go to the most extreme situation which for us would have been having the twins and ask, could we do it? Well, I felt that we could! Remember, this is coming from the guy who told our home study provider that not much would change once we had a kid. I went through all kinds of thoughts from incredibly serious to of course the idea of twins meant we had 40% of a basketball team in our own family.

I know some friends with twins, and they seem to be fine. On the other hand, I would go to the baby in Florida, and realize that I would be completely cool with that situation also. It had been a really long time since I was caught up in the idea of hoping someone liked me. I kept going back to thinking about what the birth mom may be looking for. Was my income enough? I knew there were much older people applying who made much more money. Would she think I was too short? (yes a short person has these thoughts) Would she not want us to raise her biological child to play sports? You know, the really important things.

There are tons of things that must matter to them. Now I

am about to give you some thoughts that crossed my mind, and this may be the interesting trip into my mind that you have been allowed on so far. But here are some real thoughts I had during the week we waited:

Could they tell from the picture I'm short? Does it come across in the picture how awesome Aly is? Will they know that I'm a guy that will most likely have many jobs over my lifetime? Can they tell from the pictures that I have failed?

Failed at businesses, friendships and other things. Do they realize through a picture how awesome our families are? Can they see through a picture that this child will laugh all the time? Does our picture convey our story? Does it show that we will not quit? And then of course were the questions that concerned Aly that had mostly to do with wondering if they would know she was a cancer survivor and if that would completely disqualify any birth parent from choosing us. I didn't think about that. I mean, we're awesome! But, that really worried her.

Surely we stick out in a crowd, in a good way. I felt like I was back in high school and was desperate for someone to actually know me through a small picture. That was the last time in my life that I truly remember thinking I had nothing to do with the fact that someone may pick to like me or not.

Those are most of the thoughts I remember thinking that week. Simply put, I wanted to be picked first. I wanted to be on the good team. I wanted to be wanted. I did not want to be left standing when everyone else had been picked.

Adoption Risks

Risks of the adoption process are too many to number. I'll talk about the financial risk first and how we dealt with it. Aly and I knew going in that this would not be cheap. No matter how we came across the funds, there would be immense costs in this process.

Let me first say we live in abundance. Period.

My version of abundance is not an amount of income. Abundance in my opinion has to do with worry and the worst-case scenario. For Aly and I, we have not had to worry about money for the most part. We came out of the gates into marriage blessed by our parents. We had no car notes, school loans, and a brand new car for Aly's graduation. And by no worry, I do not mean that we have had a lot of money. We just know that if we needed help, we could get it. We have people in our life that would help us financially if we need it. Thank goodness we haven't had to ask for it, outside of adoption costs, but we realize that other people do not have that available to them and that is an incredible blessing, especially for a man and husband.

We have been able to avoid credit card debt. We have certainly had rough times. I was laid off. We have lost money on a house project. Aly was in school the first 8 years we were married. Needless to say, we were not raking in the dough, but we have never gone without. To me, abundance is being taken care of, and we have been more than taken care of. Aly even graduated with her doctorate in May of 2014.

When I ventured off into real estate I developed a train of thought that looked at a situation and evaluated it at it's worst. If I can make it and this goes as poorly as possible, then we will go with it. I am not sure that is the best way to approach life situations, but that is the way Josh Taylor's mind works. This is how I tend to approach life. Sometimes that is good, and other times it can cause we to have bouts of disbelief, but that is what I naturally tend to go toward.

Our worst-case scenario is this: We move in with one of our parents if we were to have nothing while I find a job. I can dig ditches, carry shingles, tote bricks, clean windows and wash toilets like a champ. That is what I consider abundance.

Take our worst-case scenario and put it in comparison to a homeless family or someone without a family or church family, and needless to say, we look like kings.

Side bar- As I write this chapter of the book Aly and I are at a Starbucks in Honolulu. We just visited the Pier 38 fish auction at 5:30 in the morning. Very cool. If you have not been to Hawaii, you need to go. We were blessed to go to Hawaii with Aly's family. Instead of doing Christmas gifts this year, we all decided to take this trip together. Best.idea.ever. Remember the abundance I was talking about? Yes, this is a side effect, as Aly's family took a family trip here. However one of the elements no one tells you about is the homeless population in Hawaii. By far the most I have seen. Ever.

The tour guides tell you that the reason there are so many homeless is because nowhere else can a homeless person never be too hot or too cold? No where. Hawaii is the perfect climate for a homeless person and a great tourist area where tourists will give the homeless money and food. That was eye opening to us to see so many in need everywhere we went.

Aly and I have certainly never felt that pain. That is abundance. We are blessed beyond our wildest dreams.

So when we looked at the finances related to adoption,

we just believed God would provide. We weren't sure what that would look like. If needed, we would pay down a loan for the adoption. We have options when it comes to that. I have a good back and plenty of Saturdays. I can work. For us, we committed early that finances would not be the deciding factor of what we did.

I do understand that there are people that finances become more of a hurdle. Remember, Aly and I at the time of our adoption journey were are only 30 and 27. We made it through school with no debt. That is in large part due to our parents being financially wise and saving for us.

Another risk that comes with adoption is the choices of the birth mom. Will she do everything we would do if the baby was in Aly's belly? Probably not. Scratch that. Most definitely not. Aly eats grass and bird seed and exercises daily. I doubt the birth mother is doing that. I can hear Aly getting onto me saying that she eats dirt and bird seed. She just eats really healthy, but I kid with her that that is all she eats☺. That was a reality for us and almost any adoption agency and attorney we talked with discussed the likelihood of a birth mother not taking care of herself or the baby like Aly would have.

We just had to get past the part that most likely the baby

we adopted would be exposed to something that we hoped and prayed wouldn't have been a part of her growing in his or her birth mom's belly. We realized that our baby was out there, and we just prayed and believed that God would be protecting him or her. We obviously prayed that his or her birth mom would not be taking anything harmful to her or the baby, but if she had or was, that the baby would be protected with a shield and nothing adverse would touch our baby.

The biggest and most common risk for adoptive parents is emotional pain. Yes, the birth mother can change her mind at any point. There is no limit on this, basically. There are legal things in place and every situation is different, but so much of it is up to the birth parents. They obviously have every right to make decisions for the baby, but as a couple adopting, that was scary to us. That puts us at much risk emotionally. Aly kept asking, "Isn't there something they sign that keeps them somewhat bound to going through with the adoption?" And the answer is "Not really." It is still up to the birth mother after the baby is born of whether or not she will keep the baby. There is one moment when that child becomes ours. The time frame differs from state to state, but it is in the days after the baby is born when formal paperwork would be signed, and that was scary to think about.

As Aly and I looked at adoption and what pain could come with it, we were not excited about being hurt. I am not sure how long we mulled over the idea of being hurt in adoption. I know pretty quickly we came to the understanding that had Aly carried a baby, that she would have been exposed to emotional pain. There are women who lose babies all the time.

There are still-born children. We have friends that had twins and one of them passed away while still in the womb. Tell me that hurt isn't more than what hurt we agreed to expose ourselves to. I would love to not be hurt. I think I have made it clear that I do not desire to be in emotional pain.

What did hit me though was that I would gladly sign up for pain if it meant Aly could be pregnant. Why if I would do that would being exposed to pain through adoption be any different? The resounding answer was "It's not different." The answer was, "Josh Taylor, you will be excited about adoption as much if not more than Aly being pregnant. You just wait."

There will be a baby that is in desperate need of us. For that, I will sign up for pain. Not being a martyr. I simply want to realize I am not above emotional pain. The only way to never be emotionally hurt is to never love or hope.

That sounds like torture to me. We'll risk it.

Open Doors, Closed Doors

We only had to wait until Thursday that week for the verdict for at least one of the cases. As the phone rang, our hearts were beating out of our chest, but we found out that the birth mom in south Louisiana had not picked us. We were not going to be parents of twins, at least for now. Let me be honest. This is the one if I had placed my bets would be the one that would have picked us. There were only three applicants and from the criteria we understood she was looking for, we seemed to be the pick. That is not spoken out of hope. That is in direct relation to what we were told were her desires by the attorney.

Come to find out, the birth mother with twins had chosen at first, but then one other thing stuck out about another adoptive family. There was a unique piece of that adoptive family that was similar to the birth mom's life. She cared deeply about that piece, and that is why she picked that family. Regardless of what would happen with the baby in Florida, we were completely okay with this. We were slightly disappointed, but we had been praying for closed doors and open doors as we forged forward. This was clearly a closed door.

You obviously want to be picked. However, when we heard the "why" of why that birth mother hadn't chosen us, we were completely at peace. For us this is what we were depending on God to do when we continued to forge ahead. We consider this God showing up.

THE Call

This is (attorney). Is this Joshua Taylor? I said, "Uh, yeah."

That's what I heard when I answered my phone. I was at our apartment on that Friday afternoon. When I picked my phone up, I noticed that it was a FL number and almost put the phone down. Then it hit me what this could be. I remember thinking, "NO WAY!"

Why is this guy calling me? He should be calling Aly!

I went ahead and answered, and he asked if it was me to which of course I said yes. He quickly then said okay, hold on. He was calling Aly on the other line. All of a sudden he comes back on the phone and says, "Aly, can you hear me, Josh can you hear me?" To which we both said "Yes." He then said some incredible words, "Mr. and Mrs. Taylor, you were picked by _____." Crickets.

We apparently have great words when confronted with big news (insert sarcasm if you haven't picked up on my immense sarcasm at this point).

Neither Aly nor I said anything. Just "Wow." We were in shock that we didn't get picked out of 3 couples, but we did get picked out of 22! The attorney really didn't say anything else, and so we got off the phone. We didn't even ask anything. Thank goodness we talked with him a few hours later, because at the initial conversation, we didn't even know what to say or ask.

Aly then called me to find out where I was. I told her I was at the apartment, and she headed there.

Next, we were able to have our "WE'RE PREGNANT" moment. It was so much fun for Aly to walk in and for us be able to celebrate. We celebrated in spite of risk. This was no different for us than had Aly peed on a stick. This was incredible.

If this doesn't take you back to the moment you found out you were pregnant or an extremely joyful moment in your life and make you smile, then put this book down and think about it. For us, this was that. Pure joy.

This was baby Taylor. Alive and well and living in Florida. More fun than that, we were headed to meet our baby for the first time! Very quickly we were making arrangements to head to Florida to meet with the birth mother. Cloud 9, fo' real!

Chapter 12: We Were Matched!

She picked us! Aly and I were picked from 22 couples! I just remember thinking "Okay, this is real." We have a baby. Probably. I knew that we had to go meet the birth mom, but step number one was done. She actually picked us. The fun then started. It just so happened that we found out the day before we were going to celebrate Christmas at my parent's house.

I knew the fun was just beginning.

So it comes to Saturday morning when we would open presents with my family, and Aly had come up with a great plan on the fly. We had already made my mom a calendar with a bunch of pictures of us and our dog, Bella. This is what she had asked for. Aly figured out that we would mark the date on the calendar of when our baby was due. She decorated the whole month of march with scriptures and different colors, so that as they flipped through, they couldn't miss it.

This seemed somewhat foolproof, right? Well it turns out it wasn't quite as foolproof as we thought. That morning we go to my parent's house and Lee (my brother), Rachel (my sister-in-law) and Sulli (my niece) were already there. The plan was to have a huge breakfast and open presents. It was so hard to act normal.

Normal? We were about to tell my parents that grandkid number 3 was on the way!

After milling around and doing nothing, it was mentioned for us to go ahead and open presents. Per normal, we passed out the presents from person to person, and I got lucky enough to hand my mom her present, so I made sure it was the present on top. That way she would go ahead and open it. I didn't know how I would open presents knowing she was going to open that at some point.

So…mom ends up opening the calendar. All the while talking and saying how much she liked it. She opens it to January, then February and then BAM! Someone says something to her and she stops ONE page short! All we needed her to do was turn to March. Our baby's due date was March 22nd.

All we needed was for her to turn one more page and perfection! But, not in the cards for this moment. Things would only get funnier from here. So everyone is talking and mom hands the calendar off to dad. I am thinking "This is it." He will see it and the fun begins. Well ole' detail dad (sarcasm) starts flipping through the pages.

January.

February.

March!

April

And so on. The day was in MARCH!!!! He flipped right past it. What were we going to do? We wanted to surprise them. So we sat on it. Dad finished looking at this calendar and proceeds to hand it back to mom.

She grabs the calendar and in my only pre-planned line I said, "Hey I think you will like the March pic. That is the one you sent us of Bella." Mom looked and said, "What?" Thank goodness we just said "Yeah, look." She turns the page and the quiet happens.

You have to know this about my mom. She is a screamer and will celebrate with the best of them. However, some times the big ole crocodile tears come first. That is what happened in this situation. Weeping. Chest grabbing. Weeping. Re-reading. Weeping.

Then dad realizes something is up, and he looks, and then Lee and Rach realize something is going on. Then the fun started. Dad and mom knew there was a chance of us getting chosen (they knew we applied for these cases), but Lee and Rach didn't know we had applied. Their reactions are burned in my mind.

"NO! You're kidding. What are you talking about!" "When?" "How?" "WHAT?!?"

It became a lot of fun. We ended up opening the rest of the presents, and it was great. Better than we could have planned. All credit to Al and her "on the fly" idea.

The next piece was telling Ms. Cyd, Aly's mom. We knew that we were not going to see her for few days so we had to find a way to tell her that day. We called, and she was at the mall. So we headed out there to see if we could get her.

Who knew Kohl's was in the surprise business? We acted like we were looking at luggage and had her come over there. When she got there we were going to act like I got her a surprise that I couldn't wait to give her. It worked. Only problem was that I had a Go-Pro video camera in my hand to video her reaction.

When we told her to open her eyes she looked at me and thought she got a Go-Pro. I was holding the Go-Pro to video her reaction, not to gift her the Go- Pro! She was excited. Then I told her "No, look at the paper in Aly's hands!" It said, "We're Matched!"

There was lots of jumping in Kohl's and trying to act somewhat civil for the next few minutes. For the grandparents that read this, you know how much this moment meant to our parents. They wanted almost as bad as we did for us to be able to be parents. This day was not what we thought as far as there being no time to prepare for our announcement, but their reactions made it so much fun.

To Be or Not to Be: Should We be Excited?

Our cloud 9 was-short lived that day. We returned to our apartment to begin packing to leave for Florida the next day to meet the birth mom. At about 8:00 pm, Aly checked her email and our attorney had contacted Aly. What we read put our stomachs in knots. The birth mom was not returning the calls he was making to set up our meeting for the coming Monday morning.

Rock meet bottom. We went to bed that night with no

contact. Your mind is an incredible thing. Needless to say our minds went a long way that night. Had it already gone bad? Had she already changed her mind about us? Even though our attorney was continuing to not hear from her, it was our plan to continue on to Florida, and believe for the best. Going to bed with that in your belly is not a fun feeling. Aly couldn't sleep all night long and we both felt nauseous.

Sunday morning after church, Aly found out that the counselor had finally had made contact with the birth mom. There was a medical emergency in her family, and she wasn't able to answer her phone. This ended up being confirmed by our attorney. For us, this was our first roller coaster moment with adoption. We were so relieved to know that it looked like things were still "on" with the adoption.

We both walked away knowing that this may not be the last time that we get scared in this process. The adoption process can be the biggest roller coaster one can experience. We were continuing on with our mantra: Forge ahead.

Meeting Her

We boarded the plane out of Monroe, Louisiana on Sunday afternoon head for Florida. What an incredible moment. Our baby is states away, and if the birth mom likes us, tomorrow morning this thing moves forward. For real!

Hold on, if she likes us? Are you kidding me? That is what this has come to?

I ended up at the logical decision I believe made complete sense and gave us our best chance of being approved…

Aly would go alone. I'll stay in the car. Who wouldn't like Al? Nobody. Of course. Great plan, Josh, great plan.

Ends up that wasn't an option. I felt like I was back in high school, once again. "Please think I'm cool!" The line from the Julia Roberts' movie, Notting Hill comes to mind: "I'm just a boy standing in front of a girl asking her to "like" him." This was the case for us. Like us, please like us!!!

You would think this is my wheelhouse. Most people would think I would be great at talking to strangers. I have sold everything. Cars, candy bars, cookie dough, lawn service, signs, and sponsorships, but none of that helped me. This actually mattered. I was a nervous wreck. This woman is going to hate me. Aly is a sure bet, but I am going to implode, and this thing is down the tubes.

We arrived at the hotel, and all was good. When we woke up the next morning, the nerves were still there. After arriving at the meeting spot 2 hours early, we had a lot of time to waste. There was no sleeping in for these soon-to-be parents. This time was spent in Krispy Kreme, TJ Maxx, and then the ole trusty parking lot drive by.

We drove around for 20 minutes in a parking lot. Over and over. Every row. If that rental car had a memory, the next renter would get dizzy from all the circles. Aly kept saying, "Let's just walk in another store. We have time." But my stomach couldn't handle it. We were waiting on a text from the mental health counselor meeting with us and our birth mother. He was going to get there before us, and then tell us when we were good to come in. We were meeting at Panera Bread, one of our favorites, but let's be real- neither of us would be eating at this meeting. I did not want our birth mom to see me throw up.

Finally, for what seemed like forever, we got the text to come in the restaurant to meet the birth mother and baby. Once again, I have sold or asked for a lot of things. I have asked bankers or investors for silly amounts of money. Without blinking. And here I was, about to pass out.

As we walked up to the table and this pretty woman stood up and hugged us, I was in shock. I just belly hugged my baby. Really. My belly was the first thing to make contact with my child. This wasn't how I had it in my mind, but it was good. We sat for the next 2 hours just talking.

For the people who know me, this will be a shock. We were about an hour in, and all of a sudden the birth mom looks at me and says, "I'm not ignoring you, but I am mainly interested in your wife. You keep smiling so you must be happy and that's all I need to know." That is how little I was talking.

My wife is a machine. Literally a machine. It's one thing to be able to talk to a stranger. It is another thing all together to be able to connect to a stranger. Where they are and in the way they need. Yes, Al is highly educated and received her Ph.D. This-- meeting a woman carrying your baby and connecting with her in a way I've never known or seen-- however isn't taught.

Love and connection isn't something a book can teach. How can two women with such different lives and backgrounds connect like this? In that moment or I guess in those hours, I sat in awe as I watched my wife connect with a woman that was uttering words that at the same time broke our heart for her but were the reason behind her choosing to place her child with us through adoption.

One of the cries of my heart is to be better. The more I am around people that are far better than me in certain areas, the closer I get to understanding what I need to do better. I want to love people more. I want to connect better. I want anyone I speak with to understand they matter to me. Whether they are doing anything for me or not, they matter. Meeting with the birth mother made that cry of my heart much louder.

At the end of this meeting, we were able to take some pictures and Aly was even able to touch the birth mom's belly and touch our child.

What a moment. It is one we will never forget and tell our daughter about over and over and over.

Chapter 13: Waiting to Meet Our Daughter

Next, we ventured into the waiting. We were ready to see baby Taylor, but we were having so little to do with this side of her life. There were real fears with this process. It would put me at complete ease to know that our child was in Aly's belly. I know my wife and have complete confidence in her care for her body. I completely trust her and what she would expose our child to.

Having our baby girl in another woman's body brings in another set of worries. The reason that the birth mother is choosing to let us raise the daughter she is carrying is because of where she is in life. Once again, we hurt for her but are so thankful for her choosing life. That being said, there are some risks that our child will be exposed to that with us, she just simply wouldn't.

We had faith and belief that God would protect our unborn child. We had to believe that this was no different than the belief we had to have during Aly's treatment. I believe that God is for us. He is for our baby. He has had every piece of our life and our children's lives planned out before we were ever born.

I wish that I knew exactly was going into our daughter's birth mom. I know that Aly has an incredibly healthy diet. One of the worries that could easily surface is a desire to have input in our birth mom's life in these areas. What Aly and I also know is that there are children born all over this earth every day that should never be healthy. However, many are 100% good to go. We are believing that will be the case with this little girl. But it was scary, really scary at times.

Money Matters, But Does It?

What is money to you? As I have described, money to me was security. It gave me the ability to expose Aly and me to risk.

As we approved the first big chunk of money to be charged for the adoption, I felt that pit in my stomach. At that moment, I feel the rush of change that has happened in my life in the last few years. My heart has been altered by this process of cancer, infertility, and now adoption. I could not take the cancer from my wife's body. I cannot make her ovaries kick into gear and produce healthy eggs. And I cannot have control over the health of our unborn baby growing in another woman's body.

I can, however, trust that God works everything together for our good. Trusting that we have been walking in His will makes the money matter so much less. I felt that we were doing what we are supposed to do. The money is a piece of that. What I know is this. My friend, Michael, had an intense fear for the life of his unborn daughter just months ago. He and his wife were told many scary things about a possible birth defect and an emergency surgery that would have to take place right after his daughter was born.

Ask him if money mattered one ounce to him. I can guarantee his answer would be "Absolutely no." He would give everything he had for her health. For the opportunity to love her. No matter the outcome. A simple chance to love her. My bet is that his prayer was, "God, please let her arrive and breathe, and we will fight the rest." I can promise you if you had offered him the opportunity to be a dad to this little girl, he would have forked over limitless amounts of money.

How is my fear or risk any different? It's not. So yes there is risk that the birth mother could have a change of heart.

Here's a thought though. Let's say that happens. What if the birth mom needed to come across Aly and I to save the life of her baby? Was my risk of money worth it? Was my risk of money worth her seeing Jesus through us? I just don't see a negative to this.

I can work to recover the money through labor. Therefore, to me, it is not a real problem. And that is a Jesus-work in me, because let's just say I would not have felt this way before Aly's cancer diagnosis. It just puts so many things in perspective.

Let me say as a bit of disclaimer. I have operated in a world with real estate that almost each deal we did could have sunk us financially if it went wrong. When you are exposed to this level of risk, you get a little cold toward it.

Secondly, let me say that when I came face to face with the fact that money couldn't heal my wife, I was forever altered how I looked at money. Money was my security. I am just not there anymore. There are only so many things we can really control. And even as I write that, I know that isn't true, as God even controls that! Oh, the freedom there is in surrender.

I want to be in God's will. I want to be wise. My bet is

that He will take care of us. Maybe not give us billions, but certainly keep us safe and sound. We have always had more than we need.

Emotions that Come with Adoption

I am emotional. Like, I am seriously the girl in mine and Aly's relationship. When we were dating, Aly would ask me if I was on my period. I am super moody and can usually cry at the drop of a hat. Although I have gotten better, it is the truth. Al is a rock. When I am not emotionally healthy, life can be interesting. My emotions going into adoption were not totally sold on the idea. Like I said earlier, there was a piece of me that felt until we went all the way down fertility treatments that we were giving up on God moving on our behalf, since we believed He would protect Aly's womb through cancer treatment. I wanted to make sure that God knew that we truly had believed that He protected Aly's womb, and I was scared that God thought we didn't think He could actually do it, so I battled with that.

There are two distinct moments where I knew God had moved my heart to adoption, and we knew this was how God would grow our family.

When Al walked in my office and told me there was a

young couple in Alabama that had an unplanned pregnancy, I had no check up at all. My first and only thought was, "Where and when? What do we need to do to qualify for that baby?" Very quickly we found out that it wasn't quite as sure as we would like. It wasn't sure because the couple ended up getting married and keeping the baby. Awesome! We were truly happy for them. And we were happy for their potential adoption because it was a moment for us.

That moment solidified in both of us of believing that it was time. We were ready.

I remember the other moment where I truly know that God spoke to me about adoption. I was being super guarded about adoption opportunities. Had God not spoke to me, we would not have told people about the birth mom in Florida until we had met her and signed the papers. That is not a maybe. That is fact. I was scared to say anything publically to anyone in case things fell through.

About a week before our adoption opportunity came to us, I heard clearly from God that I was wrong in an area. It was key that Aly would experience pregnancy, as I explained. Even if that meant both the fun and the possible hurt. In the weeks following this, it had become such a God-confirmation as I have been able to watch my wife celebrate this coming baby girl.

Let me also say that it has allowed me to practice once again begin willing to open my heart to hurt. I am not fond of hurt. One of the big things God has done through me is made me so willing to expose myself to hurt because without the element of pain, you can't experience the fullness of joy.

Think about the happiest moments in your life and chances are that had it not gone the way it did, you would have been incredibly hurt. I have to continually be willing to expose myself to hurt so that I can experience the kind of joy God wants for me.

What I continually go back to and what in the end allows me to somewhat continue with life is that we are trusting God. We have no option but to trust God. Our worry does nothing for anything we could fret about. In our life God has shown up so big that trust comes a little quicker. If you are not awesome at believing in God and His care for your details, then I challenge you to do this little exercise.

Fill in these blanks:

God, I trust you to take care of _____ .

God, I am worried but I trust you care about

_____ way more than I do. God, My faith is so small when it comes to

_____.

Fill in those blanks. Then say it out loud.

You let your worry see the light of day, and that is not good for worry. Sometimes the worst thing we can do is allow these types of things stay in the dark. Never said, never written. You will be blown away what this does. Simply saying what you are struggling to believe God for can cause a breakthrough and you will literally feel chains released.

Here is another exercise that will help you realize how worthwhile God is when it comes to your faith and trust in him. Name the 3 biggest blessings of your life.

_____

_____

_____

Could you have created or made happen those things above? Whether those are people, things or events? You absolutely could not have made that happen with your own ability, without God giving you gifts or His amazing power and plan for it to actually happen.

So, you just listed the 3 greatest things in your life that

has happened. A God who loves you and does miracles did these things for *you*. You aren't smart enough to do it yourself. If He can do things that big, then how ridiculous would it be for you to not trust God in the other things you are hoping for.

I am continually reminded of this. When I have things in my life I am worried about or I realize I haven't fully given to God, I just have to look at my wife, or the biggest blessings in my life, and then I am back. I then realize that God can do anything. He healed my wife. He can do anything.

Find that miracle that you can look to, and know that if God can do _____, He can do anything.

Coming Full Circle

How crazy that the thought and fun I had put toward adoption as a young boy has come full circle. I sit here writing this thinking of our unborn little girl. I literally cannot wait to see her.

I challenge you to keep believing. Just be okay when you arrive at your dream on a different boat than you had planned.

My dream was to be a husband to a woman like Aly.

My other dream is to be a dad. Genevieve Rose Taylor is my dream fulfilled.

So is God worth trusting? I'll say so. He knew my heart needed to be shaped to be ready for this little girl.

She has no idea that she is the tangible piece of our heart that we didn't know how we would receive. She's about to be here, and I am ready.

My promise to my daughter yet to be born:

Genevieve Rose Taylor,

It is January 9th, 2015. I commit to becoming everything God has destined me to be. I will submit my heart to God and pray that he enables me to love your mom, Aly with everything within me. There will then be plenty of me left to love you like crazy. I love you and am so ready to meet you.

Love you forever,

Daddy

Why God changed me when he did

God's timing is always perfect. Growing up, I heard that said often. I even said it time to time, but it isn't until someone tells you that in a hard time that you want to punch them in the face! But never before in my life have I seen that play out as it has right now. This entire book was written before my first daughter was born. As I stated, the reason God healed me when he did, was to prepare me to be first, the man of God I was created to be, then love Aly like Christ loves His church, and then it was to prepare me to be the dad that Genevieve needed.

Genevieve was born on March 12, 2015, and although her adoption almost failed, a miracle happened and her birth mother chose us, and she is the most amazing little girl. I fall short every day as a man and as a father, but I wonder if God had not radically healed me like He had, what kind of dad I would be. Would I still be chasing my identity in a million other places than the One who created me? I honestly don't know the answer to that, but I am so thankful I am not who I used to be.

After Genevieve was born, 9 months later, Aly became miraculously pregnant after we were told it was impossible to get pregnant. After our failed IVF treatment, Aly was matched with an egg donor and our fertility specialist informed us that this was the only way we could get pregnant. Wow, are we thankful he was wrong!

Then one month after Aly learned she was pregnant, we found out that Genevieve's birth mother was pregnant again and asked if we would adopt that baby. The baby Aly was carrying and the baby the birth mother was carrying were due just two weeks apart. So, after much prayer, we said YES! We were basically having twins!

I am now a dad to three girls and I am literally living the dream. There are many earthly worries that we have, but every day is a good day. I am not ruled by my situation anymore and I rarely have my ups and downs because my faith is firm and I am so thankful to have my wife and my girls. Every day I see literal evidence of God's healing in my wife living and being healthy and I am face to face each day with the man I look at in the mirror and I am so thankful it is a different man after being healed through Aly's cancer.

We have several more books in the making that describe all of our miracle girls in detail, because believe me, they all deserve their own personal books with the incredible things that have happened, but I just want to leave you with this picture: When Aly was diagnosed with cancer--when God healed *her*--when God healed *me*, He knew how we would have all of our daughters and what He needed to do in us to be the parents to them they so desperately needed. I am so thankful the Lord sees the whole picture, and that we don't. It wouldn't take faith if we could see the ending. Trust with me.

So, please be encouraged. You have no clue what God is doing. Why you are walking through a valley right now--- why you are having to be broken in order to be healed. You will soon see.

It will very soon make sense, and until it does, and if it never does this side of eternity, keep willing to be broken and healed over and over and over again. The fulfillment that comes on the other side is something indescribable. I hate that it took my wife's cancer to heal me, but it did.

I am forever indebted and grateful that when God healed my wife of breast cancer, He healed me too.

God has since blessed Josh and Aly with a miracle baby conceived naturally, and another baby through adoption by Genevieve's birth mother. They are in the process of writing a book to tell their entire story of all 3 girls, but felt like they still needed to share this book that was written prior to their girls being born and how God prepared Josh's heart to be a dad of 3 girls. Stay tuned for many more books of their story and proclaiming God's goodness!

Where are we now, and why is this book being printed?

Today is July 30, 2017 and I am honestly scared to death to let this book go out. 90% of what you have read or are about to read was written before Genevieve was born.

So much more life has happened since then that I would love to tell you about. The reality is though there will be other books. I will have the opportunity to dive deeper into the details that I wish I could in this book.

Why write this book?

Because men and women need to see someone trying to live their life for Jesus. Too many incredible stories are trapped in peoples minds and computers and they cheating others of hope. I can't help everybody but if any piece of content in this book helps one person then it was worth every moment Aly and I spent making it happen.

Acknowledgements

You don't have the time or interest to see all the people that are owed thanks for getting this portion of the Taylor family to where we are today. Many people ask me what has made me able to deal with Aly having cancer, infertility, adoption, pregnancy, adoption etc? My answer is and always will be Jesus Christ. Outside of that though we would be quick to answer the family and friends we have been given.

My parents, Terry and Renea Taylor have and are walking out the Bible through the most difficult situation I can think of this side of death.

Mom and Dad, Thank you so much for fighting. Not for fighting against anyone or anything but fighting to keep your life in line with the Bible at all costs. Right now it can feel bloody and like a million little deaths but know there are lives being changed by watching you fight for God's Kingdom here on earth.

Joey and Cyd, I could not have asked for a better set of in-laws. One thing has become crystal clear through you Mrs. Cyd – one should never try and quiet their greatest fan, because there will be plenty of negative from everywhere else! We love you.

Joey, Thank you for playing a role in our lives that no one else could. You have single handedly given me the ability to be a better husband and fiercely fight for my family. Thank you.

Special thank you to Regi Cambell and RadicalMentoring (radicalmentoring.com) Thanks to Michael Hyatt, I came across your system for mentoring. Your system for mentoring and pouring into the lives of men will be my passion for the rest of my life. Thank you.

To our endless amount of incredible friends, We don't deserve you. Prayers, Time, Money. You gave us the ability to be open to what God wanted to do in our lives through fire and refinement. You eliminated so many potential problems through your love of us. You allowed us to not be distracted by the worries of this world while we fought for Aly's life and then our children.

To my mentors: Dad, Richard Jr. Martin West, Jeff Worley Ron Scott, Richard Sr, Lonnie Sr, Pastor O'Neal---It should be considered cheating to have men like this that believe in you. This is an area of life where I had it made.

To my mentees: Dylan Ogle, Cory Walker, Cody Jordan, Logan Baugh, William Fulton, Jason Hinton, Case Goodfellow, Michael Fox, Chris Ferchaud, One of the greatest gifts I have been given is the opportunity to be with you guys through Radical Mentoring. Thank you.

To the Stanfills: Our Houston family literally became family. I can't wait for the girls to know you and am so thankful to be a part of your family.

My gratitude and telling stories of how people have shaped me into who I am today and how that has produced the writing of this book---that wouldn't be a book, but a series! Wow, I am so grateful and blessed to have the most incredible people in my life.

Made in the USA
Middletown, DE
08 August 2017